Country Weekend Knits

Country Weekend Knits

25 classic patterns for timeless knitwear

Madeline Weston

jacqui small

Country Living

MAGAZINE

First published in 2008 by Jacqui Small LLP
An imprint of Aurum Press Ltd
7 Greenland Street
London NW1 0ND

ISBN: 978 1 906417 116

A catalogue record for this book is available from the
British Library.

2010 2009 2008
10 9 8 7 6 5 4 3 2 1

Printed in Singapore

Publisher Jacqui Small
Managing Editor Lesley Felce
Project Editor Zia Mattocks
Art Director Isabel de Cordova
Production Peter Colley

Photographer's Assistant Heather Lewin
Studio Photographer Sian Irvine
Studio Photographer's Assistant Joe Giacomet
Stylist Stella Nicholaisen
Hair & Make up Sharon Ive

BMA Agency models Alla Sheptunova, Tralee Dunn, Alex Preston,
Ali Zhanelova, Andy Young, Gemma Collingwood, Hannah Saunders

Locations
Knutchurch Estate
Ponttrilas, Hereford HR2 0DB – www.kentchurchcourrt.co.uk
Inglenook Camping Site
Hunstanton, Norfolk – trevor.arnold2@btinternet.com
Jeff Renant Farm
Wren Cottage, Kirk gate Street, Norfolk

Contents

Introduction

When I opened The Scottish Merchant in 1970 in London's Covent Garden, in partnership with my husband David Tomlinson, I had no idea that I would become fascinated by traditional knitting or the slightest bit knowledgeable on the subject. The shop was originally a showcase for the best of Scottish crafts, including jewellery, glass, pottery and textiles.

During the first year, we were introduced – through the artist Peggy Angus – to Margaret Stuart, who lived in Shetland. Margaret had a collection of old Fair Isle knitting, which had belonged to her grandmother and mother, and she was determined that the knitting heritage of the Shetland Islands would not disappear. She sent us a parcel of knitwear for our shop. I can still recall the excitement when we opened the first box, which contained pale, delicately knitted shawls and scarves, and vibrantly coloured Fair Isle hats, scarves and sweaters.

The Fair Isle knitwear that was available at this time was mainly in pastel colours; in particular, sweaters with round star-patterned yokes were popular. The difference between these and the items Margaret sent us was enormous. We had never seen anything like her knitwear before and – as soon became obvious – neither had our customers, who were also amazed. By using the old patterns, with their strong bands, and the traditional colours originally obtained from vegetable dyes, Margaret's group of knitters were producing knitwear that was traditional and yet fashionable. Since Margaret was also a graduate of the Royal College of Art, her colour sense was exceptional, and the shawls she supplied us reflected the lovely heather colours of Shetland.

We soon found other gems of traditional knitting in Scotland. We were approached by the parish priest of the remote isle of Eriskay in the Outer Hebrides, asking if we would be an outlet for the local knitters. There were only about a dozen knitters, and each of their ganseys took several weeks to knit. The sample that accompanied his letter was a masterpiece of patterning and construction. It was knitted in one piece, without seams, in a fine, tightly-spun worsted wool, and was covered with textured stitch patterns with enchanting names such as Marriage Lines and Tree of Life. The Eriskay gansey was immediately featured by *Harpers & Queen* magazine – then one of the world's ultimate style bibles.

At this time, young knitwear designers began to work with colour and pattern in a fresh way. Many of the now famous and established names were then exploring different approaches to knitting, and one journalist rightly called this the time of 'the knitwear revolution'. This book sets out some of the old patterns from Scotland and other parts of the British Isles, along with designers' interpretations of them. The bold cables of Aran knitting and the subtle stitch patterns of ganseys are used here in a range of yarn weights, from fine mercerised cotton to robust Aran-weight yarn for lacy cotton summer tops and chunky sweaters and jackets.

Preparing this book has brought back happy memories of running the shop in Covent Garden and long summer evenings in Shetland, and spurred the renewal of old friendships. I am happy to introduce these classic and timeless patterns, and hope you enjoy creating and wearing garments that have a direct link to the heritage of one of our oldest crafts.

Ganseys

The origins of the gansey, the traditional fishermen's sweater, go back to Elizabethan times, when an enormous number of knitted garments were exported from the Channel Islands, Jersey and Guernsey. The word 'gansey' may be derived from Guernsey, but there are marked differences between the Guernsey sweater and ganseys from other areas. The Guernsey is almost plain, and the sleeves are sewn in, whereas ganseys are often heavily patterned and free of any seams.

The gansey is similar throughout Britain, in its seamless construction, and its yarn, which is a hard 4- or 5-ply worsted, usually navy blue. However, there are huge variations in pattern from one area to another; patterns were not written down but were passed to mother to daughter, and would be constantly invented and altered. The Scottish 'lassies' who gutted the fish travelled south from Shetland during the herring-fishing season, down the coast to Norfolk, providing the workforce needed there. Old photographs taken in the middle of the nineteenth century show fishermen wearing their ganseys, and the women knitting as they walked along the quayside at the end of their working day.

The distinctive features of the gansey arose from the need to produce a practical, hardwearing garment that could be decorated with fancy stitches; because it was a working garment, it was given additional width beneath the armholes by the use of gussets. These allow ease of movement and prevent the garment from riding up. The cast-on at the rib and welt were often worked in a double thickness of wool for additional strength.

The shoulder seams were joined by knitting the front and back together and casting off at the same time; this forms an attractive ridge at the top of the shoulder.

Sometimes this would be inside the garment, with a 'shoulder strap' of contrasting pattern knitted on one side of the join. The heavier stitch pattern that appears on the chest part of the gansey gives warmth where it is needed, but the sleeves were often totally or partially plain. These were worked by picking up the stitches at the sides of the armholes and knitting down towards the cuff, so they could be unravelled and reknitted when worn out. Old ganseys in various museums often show yarn of a completely different shade halfway down the sleeves where this repair has been made.

Because they were knitting in the round, the knitters always had the pattern facing them. In order to help calculate the position of the gusset and the stitch patterns, the knitter would often work two purl stitches in the stocking stitch on either side of the body. Called 'seam stitches', these often continue down the underside of the sleeve.

The closeness of the knitting and the tightly spun worsted wool combine to make a nearly waterproof and windproof garment which could be decorated with stitch patterns to satisfy the creative imagination of the knitter. Some of these represent things important to the everyday life of the fishing community: Anchor, Harbour Steps, Cable, Fish Net. Others are more emotive: Marriage Lines, Tree of Life and Heart in Home.

The ganseys knitted by the wives for their menfolk were labours of love; the women could indulge their pride in their craft and produce an enormous variety of patterns from just knit and purl stitches. The men had their Sunday-best ganseys, which they would wear to church. In Cornwall a young bride would knit her future husband an elaborately patterned gansey called a 'bridal shirt'.

After the Industrial Revolution, when knitting frames largely replaced the hand-knitters, only the more remote areas continued to produce their hand-knitted garments. By the 1930s, the skills and patterns were fast disappearing; however, it would be only a little while before interested researchers would begin collecting patterns and old photographs to prevent this craft from dying out completely. The knitters of Eriskay, in the Outer Hebrides, are one of the last groups of women whose elaborately patterned ganseys still have the importance in the community that they did in many different fishing communities years ago.

Flamborough Fisherman's Gansey

This patterned gansey is knitted in the traditional way, on a circular needle, so there is no sewing to be done at the end. It is based on a gansey belonging to George Mainprize, who was born in about 1875 in the village of Flamborough, on the Yorkshire coast.

Polperro Pattern Jacket

This warm Shetland wool jacket is beautifully patterned with chevron and moss stitch panels copied from a gansey worn in the picturesque fishing village of Polperro, Cornwall, around 1840. It has an easy and comfortable fit, and it can be buttoned to suit a woman or a man.

Newbiggin Pattern Sweater

Vertical panels of diamonds in plain and purl stitches decorate this generously sized sweater. The pattern originates in the fishing village of Newbiggin, on the Northumberland coast, and is here knitted in an Aran-weight, soft Shetland yarn.

Short-Sleeve Cotton Shirt

The texture of this stylish but simple shirt is provided by a variation of the Broken Diamonds pattern – a traditional gansey stitch. The crisp cotton double knitting yarn used here enhances the design, but another yarn of a similar thickness may be used instead.

Jacob's Ladder Sweater

This pretty summer sweater features a saddle shoulder and traditional gansey stitches. There is a central panel of delicate cables and a Jacob's ladder pattern, which is also repeated on the sleeves. Knitted in 4-ply cotton yarn, it could also be made in another yarn of the same weight.

Fife Banded Gansey

A simple version of an old classic – found as far afield as Scotland and Cornwall – this banded gansey has a yoke decorated with garter and seed stitches. The buttoned neck is typical of a Scottish gansey. Double knitting yarn makes a soft sweater, which also knits up quickly.

Sanquhar Gansey

The black and white knitting of Sanquhar, in Dumfriesshire, Scotland, has been incorporated in this warm sweater designed by a gansey knitter. This is called the Duke's Pattern and, like similar designs, was used to embellish the fine stockings and gloves for which the town was famous.

Eriskay Gansey

The Eriskay gansey is the most intricately patterned of all ganseys, originating from the tiny Gaelic-speaking island of Eriskay, south of South Uist, in the Western Isles of Scotland. Its patterns reflect the life of the fishermen: fishing nets, waves, anchor, horseshoe, cables and starfish.

Caister Fisherman's Gansey

This traditional Norfolk gansey has a yoke patterned with seed stitches above a band of 'rig and furrow'; this stitch is repeated on the shoulder straps. The cables are unusual in having garter stitch panels at each side, which makes them stand out in high relief.

Flamborough Fisherman's Gansey

❄ MATERIALS

Yarn

7 [8, 9, 10, 11] x 100g balls Frangipani 5-ply Guernsey wool (100% wool, approx 225m/245 yards, shade Denim (also available in 500g cones, approx 1130m/1240 yards)

Needles

1 circular needle size 3mm, 80cm long

1 set of four double-pointed needles size 3mm

Notions

2 stitch holders

Special abbreviation

m1 Pick up loop lying between sts and k tbl

❄ MEASUREMENTS

To fit chest 91 [97, 102, 107, 112]cm
36 [38, 40, 42, 44]in

Actual chest size 100 [105, 109, 113, 118]cm 39¼ [41¼, 43, 44½, 46½]in

Length to back neck 61 [62, 65, 66, 68]cm
24 [24¼, 25½, 26, 26¾]in

Sleeve seam 46 [47, 49, 50, 52]cm
18 [18½, 19¼, 19¾, 20½]in

Tension

28 sts and 38 rows measure 10cm over stocking stitch on 3mm needles (or size needed to obtain given tension)

BACK AND FRONT

This garment is knitted in one piece to the armholes. Using circular needle size 3mm, cast on 264 [272, 288, 296, 312] sts. Work in rounds as follows:

Round 1 (P1, k2, p1) to end.

Rep last round until rib measures 8 [8, 9, 9, 10]cm.

Next round **P1, k13 [12, 11, 8, 9], *inc in next st, k12 [10, 14, 12, 16]; rep from * 7 [9, 7, 9, 7] times more, inc in next st, k12 [11, 10, 7, 8], p1; rep from ** once more. *282 [294, 306, 318, 330] sts.*

Next round *P1, k139 [145, 151, 157, 163], p1; rep from * once more.

Rep last round 10 times more. Commence patt.

Round 1 **P1, k13, *p8 [9, 10, 11, 12], k13; rep from * 5 times more, p1; rep from ** once more.

Round 2 **(P1, k6) twice, *p2, k4 [5, 6, 7, 8], p2, k6, p1, k6; rep from * 5 times more, p1; rep from ** once more.

Round 3 **P1, k5, p1, k1, p1, k5, *p2, k4 (5, 6, 7, 8], p2, k5, p1, k1, p1, k5; rep from * 5 times more, p1; rep from ** once more.

Round 4 **P1, k4, (p1, k1) twice, p1, k4, *p2, k4 [5, 6, 7, 8], p2, k4, (p1, k1) twice, p1, k4; rep from * 5 times more, p1; rep from ** once more.

Round 5 **P1, k3, (p1, k1) 3 times, p1, k3, *p2, k4 [5, 6, 7, 8], p2, k3, (p1, k1) 3 times, p1, k3; rep from * 5 times more, p1; rep from ** once more.

Round 6 **P1, k2, (p1, k1) 4 times, p1, k2, *p2, k4 [5, 6, 7, 8], p2, k2, (p1, k1) 4 times, p1, k2; rep from * 5 times more, p1; rep from ** once more.

Round 7 **(P1, k1) 7 times, *p2, k4 [5, 6, 7, 8], p2, k1, (p1, k1) 6 times; rep from * 5 times more, p1; rep from ** once more.

Round 8 As round 6.

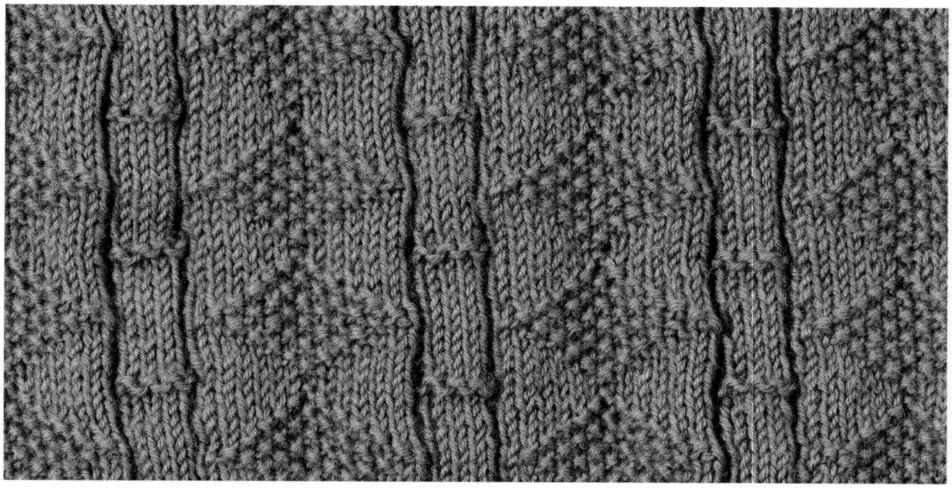

Round 9 As round 5.

Round 10 As round 4.

Round 11 As round 3.

Round 12 As round 2.

These 12 rounds form patt. Cont in patt until work measures 36 [36, 37, 37, 38]cm from beg, ending with round 12.

Shape for gusset

Next round *P1, patt 139 [145, 151, 157, 163], p1, m1; rep from * once more.

Next round *P1, patt 139 [145, 151, 157, 163], p1, k1; rep from * once more.

Next round *P1, patt 139 [145, 151, 157, 163], p1, m1, k1, m1; rep from * once more.

Next round *P1, patt 139 [145, 151, 157, 163], p1, k3; rep from * once more.

Cont in this way, inc 1 st at each end of each gusset on next round and every foll alt round until the round '*p1, patt 139 [145, 151, 157, 163], p1, k21; rep from * once more' has been worked.

Work a further 2 rounds.

Divide for front

Next round P1, m1, patt 139 [145, 151, 157, 163], m1 and turn; leave rem sts on needle.

Work backwards and forwards.

Next row (K1, p6) twice, *k2, p4 [5, 6, 7, 8], k2, p6, k1, p6; rep from * 5 times more, k1 and turn; leave rem sts on needle.

***Cont in patt as follows:

Row 1 K6, p1, k1, p1, k5, *p2, k4 [5, 6, 7, 8], p2, k5, p1, k1, p1, k5; rep from * 5 times more, k1.

Row 2 K1, p4, (k1, p1) twice, k1, p4, *k2, p4 [5, 6, 7, 8], k2, p4, (k1, p1) twice, k1, p4; rep from * 5 times more, k1.

Row 3 K4, (p1, k1) 3 times, p1, k3, *p2, k4 [5, 6, 7, 8], p2, k3, (p1, k1) 3 times, p1, k3; rep from * 5 times more, k1.

Row 4 K1, p2, (k1, p1) 4 times, k1, p2, *k2, p4 [5, 6, 7, 8], k2, p2, (k1, p1) 4 times, k1, p2; rep from * 5 times more, k1.

Row 5 K2, (p1, k1) 6 times, *p2, k4 [5, 6, 7, 8], p2, k1, (p1, k1) 6 times; rep from * 5 times more, k1.

Row 6 As row 4.

Row 7 As row 3.

Row 8 As row 2.

Row 9 As row 1.

Row 10 (K1, p6) twice, *k2, p4 [5, 6, 7, 8], k2, p6, k1, p6; rep from * 5 times more, k1.

Row 11 K14, *p8 [9, 10, 11, 12], k13; rep from * 5 times more, k1.

Row 12 As row 10.

These 12 rows form patt. Cont in patt until armholes measure 19 [20, 22, 23, 24]cm, ending with a wrong-side row. P 1 row***.

Shape neck

Next row P47 [49, 51, 53, 55] sts and turn; leave rem sts on needle.

Complete right front neck first.

Row 1 P1, (k1, p1) to end.

Rows 2–4 Purl.

Rep last 4 rows 4 times more then rows 1 and 2 once. Leave these sts on spare needle. With wrong side of front facing, sl centre 47 [49, 51, 53, 55] sts on to stitch holder, rejoin yarn to rem sts and p to end. Complete to match right front neck.

With right side of back facing, sl first 23 sts on to safety pin, rejoin yarn, m1, patt 139 [145, 151, 157, 163], m1 and sl last 23 sts on to safety pin. Work backwards and forwards.

Next row (K1, p6) twice, *k2, p4 [5, 6, 7, 8], k2, p6, k1, p6; rep from * 5 times more, k1. Work as given for front from *** to ***.

Join shoulders

With right sides of back and front together, cast off 47 [49, 51, 53, 55] sts, taking 1 st from each needle and working them tog.

Sl next 47 [49, 51, 53, 55] centre back sts on to stitch holder, rejoin yarn to rem sts and complete to match first shoulder.

NECKBAND

With right side facing and using set of four double-pointed needles size 3mm, pick up and k 17 sts down left front neck, k across 47 [49, 51, 53, 55] centre front sts, pick up and k 17 sts up right front neck, k across 47 [49, 51, 53, 55] centre back sts. *128 [132, 136, 140, 144] sts.* Work 11 rounds in k2, p2, rib. Cast off in rib.

SLEEVES

With right side facing and using set of four double-pointed needles size 3mm, pick up and k 121 [127, 133, 139, 145] sts evenly around armhole edge, then p1, k21, p1 sts from safety pin. *144 [150, 156, 162, 168] sts.*

Work in rounds as follows:

Next round P to last 22 sts, k21, p1.

Commence patt.

Round 1 K25 [26, 27, 28, 29], p2, k4 [5, 6, 7, 8], p2, *k6, p1, k6, p2, k4 [5, 6, 7, 8], p2; rep from * twice more, k25 [26, 27, 28, 29], p1, ybk, skpo, k17, k2 tog, p1.

Round 2 K25 [26, 27, 28, 29], p2, k4 [5, 6, 7, 8], p2, *k5, p1, k1, p1, k5, p2, k4 [5, 6, 7, 8], p2; rep from * twice more, k25 [26, 27, 28, 29], p1, k19, p1.

Round 3 K25 [26, 27, 28, 29], p2, k4 [5, 6, 7, 8], p2, *k4, (p1, k1) twice, p1, k4, p2, k4 [5, 6, 7, 8], p2; rep from * twice more, k25 [26, 27, 28, 29], p1, ybk, skpo, k15, k2 tog, p1.

Round 4 K25 [26, 27, 28, 29], p2, k4 [5, 6, 7, 8], p2, *k3, (p1, k1) 3 times, p1, k3, p2, k4 [5, 6, 7, 8], p2; rep from * twice more, k25 [26, 27, 28, 29], p1, k17, p1.

Round 5 K25 [26, 27, 28, 29], p2, k4 [5, 6, 7, 8], p2, *k2, (p1, k1) 4 times, p1, k2, p2, k4 [5, 6, 7, 8], p2; rep from * twice more, k25 [26, 27, 28, 29], p1, ybk, skpo, k13, k2 tog, p1.

Round 6 K25 [26, 27, 28, 29], p2, k4 [5, 6, 7, 8], p2, *k1, (p1, k1) 6 times, p2, k4 [5, 6, 7, 8], p2; rep from * twice more, k25 [26, 27, 28, 29], p1, k15, p1.

Round 7 K25 [26, 27, 28, 29], p2, k4 [5, 6, 7, 8], p2, *k2, (p1, k1) 4 times, p1, k2, p2, k4 [5, 6, 7, 8], p2; rep from * twice more, k25 [26, 27, 28, 29], p1, ybk, skpo, k11, k2 tog, p1.

Round 8 K25 [26, 27, 28, 29], p2, k4 [5, 6, 7, 8], p2, *k3, (p1, k1) 3 times, p1, k3, p2, k4 [5, 6, 7, 8], p2; rep from * twice more, k25 [26, 27, 28, 29], p1, k13, p1.

Round 9 K25 [26, 27, 28, 29], p2, k4 [5, 6, 7, 8], p2, *k4, (p1, k1) twice, p1, k4, p2, k4 [5, 6, 7, 8], p2; rep from * twice more, k25 [26, 27, 28, 29], p1, ybk, skpo, k9, k2 tog, p1.

Round 10 K25 [26, 27, 28, 29], p2, k4 [5, 6, 7, 8], p2, *k5, p1, k1, p1, k5, p2, k4 [5, 6, 7, 8], p2; rep from * twice more, k25 [26, 27, 28, 29], p1, k11, p1.

Round 11 K25 [26, 27, 28, 29], p2, k4 [5, 6, 7, 8], p2, *k6, p1, k6, p2, k4 [5, 6, 7, 8], p2; rep from * twice more, k25 [26, 27, 28, 29], p1, ybk, skpo, k7, k2 tog, p1.

Round 12 K25 [26, 27, 28, 29], p8 [9, 10, 11, 12], *k13, p8 [9, 10, 11, 12]; rep from * twice more, p1, k9, p1.

These 12 rounds establish patt. Cont in patt as set, dec 1 st at each end of gusset on next round and 2 foll alt rounds. Work 1 round straight.

Next round Patt 121 [127, 133, 139, 145], p1, ybk, sl 1, k2 tog, psso, p1.

Next round Patt 121 [127, 133, 139, 145], p1, k1, p1.

Next round Patt 121 [127, 133, 139, 145], p2 tog, p1.

Next round Patt 121 [127, 133, 139, 145], p2. Repeat last round twice.

Next round Skpo, patt to last 4 sts, k2 tog, p2. Rep last 4 rounds 8 times. Work 3 rounds straight.

Next round Skpo, k to last 4 sts, k2 tog, p2.
Next 3 rounds K to last 2 sts, p2.
Rep last 4 rounds until 69 [73, 77, 85, 89] sts rem. Cont straight until sleeve measures 38 [39, 40, 41, 42]cm.

Next round K7, *k2 tog, k11 [12, 13, 15, 16]; rep from * to last 10 sts, k2 tog, k6 p2. *64 [68, 72, 80, 84] sts.*
Work 8 [8, 9, 9, 10]cm in rounds of k2, p2 rib. Cast off in rib.

FINISHING

Block as given on page 139.

Polperro Pattern Jacket

❋ MATERIALS

Yarn

22 x 50g balls Jamieson's Shetland Heather Aran (100% pure Shetland wool, approx 92m/101 yards), shade 1390 Highland Mist.

Note: The yarn is used double throughout

Needles

1 pair size 6.5mm

1 pair size 7.5mm

Notions

8 buttons, 3cm in diameter

2 buttons, 2.5cm in diameter

❋ MEASUREMENTS

To fit chest 91–102 [107–116]cm

36–40 [42–46]in

Actual chest size 117 [133]cm

46 [52¼]in

Length to back neck 65 [69]cm

25½ [27]in

Sleeve seam 45 [49]cm

17¾ [19¼]in

Tension

12 sts and 18 rows measure 10cm over pattern on 7.5mm needles (or size needed to obtain given tension)

POCKET LININGS

Using 7.5mm needles and 2 strands of yarn together, cast on 13 [17] sts. Beg k row, work 12 rows in st st. Leave these sts on a spare needle. Make another pocket lining to match.

RIGHT FRONT

Woman's jacket

Using 6.5mm needles and 2 strands of yarn together, cast on 35 [41] sts.

Row 1 (Right side) K1, (p1, k1) to end.

Row 2 (P1, k1) to last 7 [9] sts, k1, (p1, k1) to end.

These 2 rows form moss st and rib patt.

Row 3 Patt 3 [4], cast off 1, patt to end.

Row 4 Patt to end, casting on 1 st over the 1 st cast off in previous row.

Rows 5–14 Rep rows 1 and 2, 5 times.

Row 15 As row 3.

Row 6 Patt 3, *inc in next st, patt 4 [5]; rep from * 3 times more, inc in next st, patt 7 [8], cast on 1, patt to end. *40 [46] sts.*

Change to 7.5mm needles. Commence main patt.

Row 1 K1, (p1, k1) 3 [4] times, *(k5, p1) twice, (k1, p1) 2 [3] times; rep from * once more, k1.

Row 2 K1, *(p1, k1) 2 [3] times, p5, k1, p1, k1, p4; rep from * once more, k1, (p1, k1) 3 [4] times.

Row 3 K1, (p1, k1) 3 [4] times, *(k3, p1) 3 times, (k1, p1) 2 [3] times; rep from * once more, k1.

Row 4 K1, *(p1, k1) 2 [3] times, p3, k1, p5, k1, p2; rep from * once more, k1, (p1, k1) 3 [4] times.

Row 5 K1, (p1, k1) 3 [4] times, *k1, p1, k7, p1, (k1, p1) 3 [4] times; rep from * once more, k1.

Row 6 K1, *(p1, k1) 3 [4] times, p9, k1; rep from * once more, k1 (p1, k1) 3 [4] times.

These 6 rows form main patt. Patt 4 [10] rows.

Next row Patt 3 [4], cast off 1, patt to end.

Next row Patt to end, casting on 1 st over the 1 st cast off in previous row.

Patt 6 [0] rows.

Place pocket

Next row Patt 14 [16], sl next 13 [17] sts on to stitch holder, patt across 13 [17] sts of pocket lining, patt to end. Cont in patt making button-holes as before on follow 10th and 11th [16th and 17th] rows and 3 foll 17th and 18th rows.

Shape neck

Next row Patt 7 [9] and sl these sts on to safety pin, patt to end.

Patt 1 row. Cast off 3 [4] sts at beg of next row. Dec 1 st at neck edge on next 2 rows then on 2 [3] foll alt rows. *26 [28] sts.*

Patt 9 [7] rows straight. Cast off.

Man's jacket

Work as given for right front of woman's jacket omitting buttonholes.

LEFT FRONT

Woman's jacket

**Using 6.5mm needles and 2 strands of yarn together, cast on 35 [41] sts.

Cheveron and moss stitch pattern

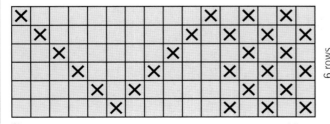

Size 1   16 sts

6 rows

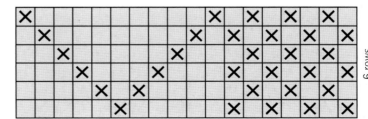

Size 2   18 sts

6 rows

Row 1 (Right side) K1, (p1, k1) to end.
Row 2 K1, (p1, k1) 3 [4] times, (k1, p1) to end.
These 2 rows form moss st and rib patt**.
Patt 13 rows.
Next row Patt 11 [13], *inc in next st, patt 4 [5]; rep from * to last 4 sts, inc in next st, patt to end. *40 [46] sts.*
***Change to 7.5mm needles. Commence main patt.
Row 1 K1, *(p1, k1) 2 [3] times, (p1, k5) twice; rep from * once more, k1, (p1, k1) 3 [4] times.
Row 2 K1, (p1, k1) 3 [4] times, *p4, k1, p1, k1, p5, (k1, p1) 2 [3] times; rep from * once more, k1.
Row 3 K1, *(p1, k1) 2 [3] times, (p1, k3) 3 times; rep from * once more, k1, (p1, k1) 3 [4] times.

Row 4 K1, (p1, k1) 3 [4] times, *p2, k1, p5, k1, p3, (k1, p1) 2 [3] times; rep from * once more, k1.
Row 5 K1, *(p1, k1) 3 [4] times, p1, k7, p1, k1; rep from * once more, k1, (p1, k1) 3 [4] times.
Row 6 K1, (p1, k1) 3 [4] times, *k1, p9, (k1, p1) 3 [4] times; rep from * once more, k1. These 6 rows form main patt***. Patt 12 rows.
Place pocket
Next row Patt 13, sl next 13 [17] sts on to stitch holder, patt across 13 [17] sts of pocket lining, patt to end. Patt 64 [70] rows.
Shape neck
Next row Patt 7 [9] and sl these sts on to safety pin, patt to end.
Patt 1 row. Cast off 3 [4] sts at beg of next

row. Dec 1 st at neck edge on next 2 rows then on 2 [3] foll alt rows. *26 [28] sts.*
Patt 10 [8] rows straight. Cast off.
Man's jacket
Work as given for left front of woman's jacket from ** to **.
Row 3 Patt to last 4 [5] sts, cast off 1, patt to end.
Row 4 Patt to end, casting on 1 st over the 1 st cast off in previous row.
Rows 5–14 Rep rows 1 and 2, 5 times.
Row 15 As row 3.
Row 16 Patt 3 [4], cast on 1, patt 7 [8], *inc in next st, patt 4 [5]; rep from * 3 times more, inc in next st, patt 3. *40 [46] sts.*

Work as given for left front of woman's jacket from *** to ***. Patt 4 [10] rows.

Next row Patt to last 4 sts, cast off 1, patt to end.

Next row Patt to end casting on 1 st over the 1 st cast off in previous row. Patt 6 [0] rows.

Place pocket

Next row Patt 13, sl next 13 [17] sts on to stitch holder, patt across 13 [17] sts of pocket lining, patt to end.

Cont in patt making buttonholes as before on foll 10th and 11th [16th and 17th] rows and 2 foll 17th and 18th rows. Patt 16 rows straight then work 1 buttonhole row.

Shape neck

Next row Patt 3 [4], cast on 1, patt 3 [4] and sl these 7 [9] sts on to safely pin, patt to end. Complete as given for left front of woman's jacket.

BACK

Using 6.5mm needles and 2 strands of yarn together, cast on 60 [70] sts. Work 15 rows in k1, p1 rib.

Next row Rib 5 [4], *inc in next st, rib 4 [5]; rep from * to end. *71 [81] sts.* Change to 7.5mm needles. Commence main patt.

Row 1 (Right side) (K1, p1) 3 [4] times, *(k5, p1) twice, (k1, p1) 2 [3] times; rep from * to last st, k1.

Row 2 (K1, p1) 3 [4] times, *p4, k1, p1, k1, p5, (k1, p1) 2 [3] times; rep from * to last st, k1.

Row 3 (K1, p1) 3 [4] times, *(k3, p1) 3 times, (k1, p1) 2 [3] times; rep from * to last st, k1.

Row 4 (K1, p1) 3 [4] times, *p2, k1, p5, k1, p3, (k1, p1) 2 [3] times; rep from * to last st, k1.

Row 5 (K1, p1) 3 [4] times, *k1, p1, k7, (p1, k1) 3 [4] times, p1; rep from * to last st, k1.

Row 6 (K1, p1) 3 [4] times, *k1, p9, (k1, p1) 3 [4] times; rep from * to last st, k1.

These 6 rows form main patt. Rep these 6 rows 16 [17] times more. Cast off.

SLEEVES

Using 6.5mm needles and 2 strands together, cast on 32 [38] sts. Work 15 rows in k1, p1 rib.

Next row Rib 4 [3], *inc in next st, rib 3 [4]; rep from * to end. *39 [45] sts.*

Change to 7.5mm needles.

Work 6 rows in patt as given for back. Cont in patt, inc 1 st at each end of next row and every foll 4th row until there are 63 [69] sts, working extra sts into st st. Work 3 [9] rows straight in patt.

Next row Inc in first st, (p1, k1) to last 2 sts, p1, inc in last st.

Next row P1, (k1, p1) to end.

Next row Inc in first st, (k1, p1) to last 2 sts, k1, inc in last st.

Next row K1, (p1, k1) to end.

Rep last 4 rows twice more. *75 [81] sts.* Cast off.

NECKBAND

Join shoulder seams. With right side facing, sl 7 [9] sts on right front safety pin on to 6.5mm needle, using 2 strands of yarn together, pick up and k 18 sts up right front neck, 21 [23] sts across back neck, 18 sts down left front neck and k1, (p1, k1) 3 [4] times from left front safety pin. *71 [77] sts.*

Row 1 (Wrong side) K1, (p1, k1) 3 [4] times, k1, (p1, k1) to last 7 [9] sts, k1, (p1, k1) 3 [4] times.

Row 2 K1, (p1, k1) to end.

These 2 rows form moss st and rib patt. Patt 1 row.

Next row Patt 3 [4], cast off 1, patt to end.

Next row Patt to end, casting on 1 st over the 1 st cast off in previous row. Patt 2 rows. Cast off in patt.

POCKET EDGINGS

With right side facing and using 7.5mm needles and 2 strands of yarn together, rejoin yarn to the 13 [17] sts on holder, (k1, p1) 3 [4] times, cast off 1, p1 (st used in casting off), (k1, p1) 2 [3] times.

Next row (K1, p1) 3 [4] times, cast on 1, (p1, k1) 3 [4] times.

Next row K1, (p1, k1) to end.

Rep last row once. Cast off.

FINISHING

Block as given on page 139. Mark position of armholes 30 [33]cm down from shoulders on back and fronts. Sew in sleeves. Join side and sleeve seams. Catch down pocket linings and sides of pocket edgings. Sew on buttons as shown, placing 2 smaller buttons at neck.

Newbiggin Pattern Sweater

❊ MATERIALS

Yarn

15 x 50g balls Jamieson and Smith's Shetland Aran (100% pure new wool, approx 90m/98 yards), shade SS11 (marine blue)

Needles

1 pair size 3.75mm

1 pair size 4.5mm

Special abbreviation

tw2 K into front of 2nd st then k first st, sl both sts off needle tog

❊ MEASUREMENTS

To fit chest 107–117cm, 42–46in

Actual chest size 126cm, 49½in

Length to back neck 68cm, 26¾in

Sleeve seam 50cm, 19¾in

Tension

17 sts and 23 rows measure 10cm over pattern on 4.5mm needles (or size needed to obtain given tension)

PATTERN PANEL

Repeat of 38 sts.

Row 1 (Right side) (P2, tw2) twice, k11, tw2, p2, tw2, p11, tw2.

Row 2 P2, k5, p1, k5, p2, k2, p7, k1, p5, (p2, k2) twice.

Row 3 (P2, tw2) twice, k4, p3, k4, tw2, p2, tw2, p4, k3, p4, tw2.

Row 4 P2, k3, p5, k3, p2, k2, p5, k5, p3, (p2, k2) twice.

Row 5 (P2, tw2) twice, k2, p7, k2, (tw2, p2) twice, k7, p2, tw2.

Row 6 P2, k1, p9, k1, p2, k2, p3, k9, p1, (p2, k2) twice.

Row 7 As row 5.

Row 8 As row 4.

Row 9 As row 3.

Row 10 As row 2.

Row 11 As row 1.

Row 12 P15, k2, p2, k11, (p2, k2) twice.

Row 13 (P2, tw2) twice, p5, k1, p5, tw2, p2, tw2, k5, p1, k5, tw2.

Row 14 P6, k3, p6, k2, p2, k4, p3, k4, (p2, k2) twice.

Row 15 (P2, tw2) twice, p3, k5, p3, tw2, p2, tw2, k3, p5, k3, tw2.

Row 16 P4, k7, p4, k2, p2, k2, p7, k2, (p2, k2) twice.

Row 17 (P2, tw2) twice, p1, k9, p1, tw2, p2, tw2, k1, p9, k1, tw2.

Row 18 As row 16.

Row 19 As row 15.

Row 20 As row 14.

Row 21 As row 13.

Row 22 As row 12.

These 22 rows form panel patt.

BACK

Using 3.75mm needles, cast on 96 sts. Work 7cm in k1, p1 rib.

Next row Rib 9, (inc in next st, rib 5) to last 3 sts, rib 3. *110 sts.*

Change to 4.5mm needles. Commence patt.

Row 1 (Right side) (K2, p2) 3 times, tw2, rep row 1 of panel patt twice, (p2, tw2) twice, (p2, k2) 3 times.

Row 2 (P2, k2) 5 times, rep row 2 of panel patt twice, p2, (k2, p2) 3 times.

Row 3 (P2, k2) 3 times, tw2, rep row 3 of panel patt twice, (p2, tw2) twice, (k2, p2) 3 times.

Row 4 (K2, p2) 3 times, (p2, k2) twice, rep row 4 of panel patt twice, p2, (p2, k2) 3 times.

These 4 rows establish patt. Cont in patt as set, working appropriate rows of panel patt until work measures 65cm from beg, ending with row 2 of panel patt.

Shape shoulders

Cast off 10 sts at beg of next 8 rows. Leave rem sts on spare needle.

FRONT

Work as given for back until front measures 61cm from beg, ending with row 14 of panel patt.

Shape neck

Next row Patt 49 and turn; leave rem sts on a spare needle. Complete left side of neck first. Dec 1 st at neck edge on next 9 rows.

Shape shoulder

Cast off 10 sts at beg of next row and 2 foll alt rows. Work 1 row. Cast off rem sts. With right side facing, sl centre 12 sts on to a safety pin, rejoin yarn to rem sts, patt to end. Complete as given for left side neck.

Diamond pattern

22 rows

11 sts

SLEEVES

Using 3.75mm needles, cast on 50 sts. Work 7cm in k1, p1 rib.
Next row Rib 2, (inc in next st, rib 3) to end. *62 sts.*
Change to 4.5mm needles. Commence patt.
Row 1 (Right side) K9, tw2, p2, tw2, p11, tw2 (p2, tw2) twice, k11, tw2, p2, tw2, p9.
Row 2 K3, p1, k5, p2, k2, p7, k1, p5, (p2, k2) twice, p2, k5, p1, k5, p2, k2, p7, k1, p3.
Row 3 K2, p3, k4, tw2, p2, tw2, p4, k3, p4, tw2, (p2, tw2) twice, k4, p3, k4, tw2, p2, tw2, p4, k3, p2.
Row 4 K1, p5, k3, p2, k2, p5, k5, p3, (p2, k2) twice, p2, k3, p5, k3, p2, k2, p5, k5, p1.
These 4 rows establish patt. Cont in patt, inc 1 st at each end of next row and 4 foll 5th rows then on every foll 6th row until there are 96 sts, working extra sts into patt. Work 3 rows straight. Cast off.

NECKBAND

Join right shoulder seam. With right side facing and using 3.75mm needles, pick up and k 19 sts down left side neck, k across 12 centre front sts, pick up and k 19 sts up right side neck, and k across 30 centre back sts. *80 sts.*
Work 6cm in k1, p1 rib. Cast off in rib.

FINISHING

Block each piece as given on page 139.
Join left shoulder and neckband seam. Fold neckband in half to wrong side and slipstitch in position. Mark positions of armholes 27cm down from shoulders on back and front.
Sew in sleeves between markers. Join side and sleeve seams.

Short-Sleeve Cotton Shirt

❋ MATERIALS

Yarn
13 [13, 14] x 50g balls Rowan handknit
cotton (100% cotton, approx 85m/93
yards), shade 251 Ecru
Needles
1 pair size 3.25mm
1 pair size 4mm
Notions
3 buttons, 1.5cm in diameter

❋ MEASUREMENTS
To fit chest 86 [91, 97]cm
34 [36, 38]in
Actual chest size 96 [100, 104]cm
38 [39, 41]in
Length to back neck 60 [61, 62]cm
23¼ [24, 24½]in
Sleeve seam 15cm, 6in
Tension
20 sts and 32 rows measure 10cm over
pattern on 4mm needles (or size needed
to obtain given tension)

BACK

Using 3.25mm needles, cast on 98 [102, 106]
sts. Work 3cm in k1, p1 rib. Change to 4mm
needles. Commence patt.
Row 1 (Wrong side) P0 [2, 4], (p4, k6, p4)
to last 0 [2, 4] sts, p0 [2, 4].
Row 2 Knit.
Rows 3 and 4 As rows 1 and 2.
Row 5 As row 1.
Row 6 K3 [5, 7], (p1, k6) to last 4 [6, 8] sts,
p1, k3 [5, 7].
Row 7 P0 [0, 1], k0 [0, 1], p0, [2, 2], (p2, k1,
p8, k1, p2) to last 0 [2, 4] sts, p0 [2, 2], k0 [0,
1], p0 [0, 1].
Row 8 K0, [0, 2], p0 [1, 1], k0 [1, 1], (k1, p1,
k10, p1, k1) to last 0 [2, 4] sts, k0 [1, 1], p0
[1, 1], k0 [0, 2].
Row 9 p0 [1, 3], k0 [1, 1], (k1, p12, k1) to
last 0 [2, 4] sts, k0 [1, 1], p0 [1, 3].

Row 10 As row 8.
Row 11 As row 7.
Row 12 As row 6.
These 12 rows form patt. Cont in patt until
work measures 60 [61, 62]cm from beg,
ending with a wrong-side row.
Shape shoulders
Cast off 34 [36, 38] sts at beg of next 2 rows.
Cast off rem 30 sts.

FRONT

Work as given for back until work measures
39 [40, 41]cm from beg, ending with a right-
side row.
Divide for neck opening.
Next row Patt 46 [48, 50], cast off 6, patt to
end. Complete left side of front first. Cont
straight until front measures 52 [53, 54]cm
from beg, ending at neck edge.

Shape neck
Cast off 6 sts at beg of next row. Dec 1 st at
neck edge on every right-side row until 34
[36, 38] sts rem. Cont straight until front
matches back to shoulder, ending at side edge.
Cast off. With right side facing, rejoin yarn
to rem sts and patt to end. Complete as given
for first side of neck.

SLEEVES

Using 3.25mm needles, cast on 70 [74, 78] sts.
Work 3cm in k1, p1 rib. Change to 4mm
needles. Cont in patt as given for back, inc
1 st at each end of 3rd row and every foll
alt row until there are 98 [102, 106] sts,
working extra sts into patt. Cont straight
until work measures 15cm from beg, ending
with a wrong-side row.
Cast off.

BUTTON BANDS

Buttonhole band

With right side facing and using 3.25mm needles, pick up and k 28 sts evenly along right side of neck opening. Work 3 rows in k1, p1 rib.

Buttonhole row
Rib 3, (cast off 2, rib 8 including st used in casting off) twice, cast off 2, rib to end.
Next row Rib to end, casting on 2 sts over those cast off in previous row.
Rib 2 rows. Cast off in rib.

Button band

Work as given for buttonhole band, picking up sts along left side of neck opening and omitting buttonholes.

COLLAR

Using 3.25mm needles, cast on 103 sts.
Row 1 (Right side) K1, (p1, k1) to end.
Row 2 P1, (k1, p1) to end.
Rep these 2 rows until collar measures 7cm, ending with a wrong-side row. Cast off in rib.

FINISHING

Block each piece as given on page 139. Overlap buttonhole band over button border and catch down at base of opening. Join shoulder seams. Sew on collar. Mark position of armholes 24 [25, 26]cm down from shoulder on back and front. Sew in sleeves between markers. Join side and sleeve seams. Sew on buttons.

Jacob's Ladder Sweater

❊ MATERIALS

Yarn
9 [10, 11] x 50g balls Rowan 4-ply cotton (100% cotton, approx 170m/186 yards), shade 135 Fennel

Needles
1 pair size 2.25mm
1 pair size 3.25mm
1 cable needle

Special abbreviations
m1 Pick up loop lying between sts and work tbl
c6f Sl next 3 sts on to cable needle and leave at front of work, k3 from left-hand needle, k3 from cable needle
c6b Sl next 3 sts on to cable needle and leave at back of work, k3 from left-hand needle, k3 from cable needle

❊ MEASUREMENTS

To fit chest 86 [91, 97]cm
34 [36, 38]in
Actual chest size 92 [100, 110]cm
36 [39½, 43½]in
Length to back neck 55 [56, 57]cm
21½ [22, 22½]in
Sleeve seam 44 [45, 46]cm
17¼ [17¾, 18]in

Tension
28 sts and 40 rows measure 10cm over stocking stitch on 3.25mm needles (or size needed to obtain given tension)

BACK

Using 2.25mm needles, cast on 109 [119, 127] sts.
Row 1 (Right side) K1, (p1, k1) to end.
Row 2 P1, (k1, p1) to end.
Rep these 2 rows until rib measures 10cm, ending with row 1.
Next row Rib 10 [12, 10], (m1, rib 3) to last 6 [8, 6] sts, rib to end. *140 [152, 164] sts.*
Change to 3.25mm needles. Commence patt.
Row 1 K45 [51, 57], k1 tbl, p2, k6, p2, k1 tbl, k26, k1 tbl, p2, k6, p2, k1 tbl, k45 [51, 57].
Row 2 P46 [52, 58], k2, p6, k2, p28, k2, p6, k2, p46 [52, 58].
Row 3 K45 [51, 57], k1 tbl, p2, c6f, p2, k1 tbl, k26, k1 tbl, p2, c6b, p2, k1 tbl, k45 [51, 57].
Row 4 As row 2.
Rows 5–8 Rep rows 1 and 2 twice.
Row 9 As row 3.
Row 10 P46 [52, 58], k2, p6, k2, p1, k26, p1, k2, p6, k2, p46 [52, 58].
Row 11 As row 1.
Row 12 As row 10.
These 12 rows form patt. Cont in patt until work measures 35 [36, 37]cm from beg, ending with a wrong-side row.

Shape armholes
Cast off 8 sts at beg of next 2 rows. Dec 1 st at each end of next row and every foll alt row until 102 [106, 110] sts rem. Cont straight until armholes measure 18cm, ending with a wrong-side row.

Shape shoulders
Cast off 8 [8, 9] sts at beg of next 6 rows and 7 [9, 8] sts at beg of foll 2 rows. Leave rem 40 sts on a spare needle.

FRONT

Work as given for back until armholes measure 13cm, ending with a wrong-side row.

Shape neck
Next row Patt 45 [47, 49] sts and turn; leave rem sts on a spare needle. Complete left side of neck first. Cast off 4 sts at beg of next row and foll alt row and 2 sts at beg of foll alt row. Dec 1 st at neck edge on foll 4 alt rows. *31 [33, 35] sts.* Cont straight until front matches back to shoulder, ending at armhole edge.

Shape shoulder
Cast off 8 [8, 9] sts at beg of next row and foll 2 alt rows. Work 1 row. Cast off rem 7 [9, 8] sts.
With right side facing, sl centre 12 sts on to a safety pin, rejoin yarn to rem sts and patt to end. Patt 1 row. Complete as given for first side of neck.

SLEEVES

Using 2.25mm needles, cast on 60 sts. Work 8cm in k1, p1 rib.
Next row Rib 4, (m1, rib 4) to end. *74 sts.*
Change to 3.25mm needles. Commence patt.
Rows 1–8 Beg with a k row, work 8 rows st st.
Rows 9–12 Knit.
These 12 rows form patt. Cont in patt, inc 1 st at each end of next row and every foll 7th

row until there are 106 sts. Cont straight until sleeve measures 44 [45, 46]cm from beg, ending with a wrong-side row.

Shape top

Cast off 8 sts at beg of next 2 rows. Dec 1 st at each end of next row and every foll alt row until 28 sts rem. Work 10 [11, 12]cm straight on these sts for saddle shoulder, ending with a wrong-side row. Leave these sts on a spare needle.

NECKBAND

Join right sleeve saddle shoulder to back and front and left sleeve saddle shoulder to front. With right side facing and using 2.25mm needles, k across 28 sts from left saddle shoulder, pick up and k 24 sts down left front neck, k across 12 centre front sts, pick up and k 24 sts up right front neck, k across 28 sts from right saddle shoulder and 40 centre back sts. *156 sts.* Work 7 rows in k1, p1 rib. Cast off in rib.

FINISHING

Block pieces as given on page 139. Join left saddle shoulder to back, then join neckband. Sew in sleeves. Join side and sleeve seams.

Fife Banded Gansey

❋ MATERIALS

Yarn
11 [12, 13, 14, 15] x 50g balls Jaeger
Matchmaker merino double knitting
(100% wool, approx 120m/131 yards)
shade 789 Syrup
Needles
1 circular needle size 3.75mm, 80cm long
1 set of double-pointed needles size
3.75mm
Notions
2 buttons, 1.5cm in diameter
2 stitch holders
Special abbreviation
m1 Pick up loop lying between sts
and k tbl

❋ MEASUREMENTS

To fit chest 91 [97, 102, 107, 112]cm
36 [38, 40, 42, 44]in
Actual chest size 102 [107, 112, 116, 121]cm
40 [42, 44, 45¾, 47¾]in
Length to back neck 59 [62, 64, 68, 70]cm
23¼ [24¼, 25¼, 26¾, 27½]in
Sleeve seam 46 [47, 48, 49, 50]cm
18 [18½, 19, 19¼, 19¾]in
Tension
26 sts and 34 rows measure 10cm over
stocking stitch on 3.75mm needles (or size
needed to obtain given tension).

BACK AND FRONT

This is knitted in one piece up to the
armholes. Using 3.75mm circular needle,
cast on 232 [240, 256, 264, 280] sts.
Work in rounds as follows:
Round 1 (K2, p2) to end of round.
Rep this round until rib measures 6 [6, 7, 7,
8]cm.
Next round **K7 [5, 8, 5, 9], *m1, k10 [9, 11,
10, 12]; rep from * 9 [11, 9, 11, 9] times more,
m1, k7 [5, 8, 5, 9], p1, m1, p1**; rep from ** to
** once more. *256 [268, 280, 292, 304] sts.*
Cont in st st as follows:
Round 1 *K125 [131, 137, 143, 149], p3; rep
from * once more.
Round 2 *K125 [131, 137, 143, 149], p1, k1,
p1; rep from * once more.
Rep these 2 rounds until work measures 31
[32, 34, 36, 38]cm from beg, ending with
round 2.
Change to yoke patt.
Round 1 Purl.
Round 2 *P126 [132, 138, 144, 150], k1, p1;
rep from * once more.
Round 3 Purl.
Round 4 *K125 [131, 137, 143, 149], p1, k1,
p1; rep from * once more.
Round 5 *K125 [131, 137, 143, 149], p3; rep
from * once more.
Round 6 As round 4.
Rep rounds 1–3.
Shape for gusset
Round 1 *K125 [131, 137, 143, 149], p1, m1,
k1, m1, p1; rep from * once more.
Round 2 *K125 [131, 137, 143, 149], p1, k3,
p1; rep from * once more.
Round 3 *K1 [0, 1, 0, 1], (p3, k1) 31 [32, 34,
35, 37] times, p0 [3, 0, 3, 0], p1, k3, p1; rep
from * once more.
Round 4 As round 2.
Round 5 *K125 [131, 137, 143, 149], p1, k1,
(m1, k1) twice, p1; rep from * once more.
Round 6 *P2 [1, 2, 1, 2], k1, (p3, k1) 30 [32,
33, 35, 36] times, p3 [2, 3, 2, 3], k5, p1; rep
from * once more.

Round 7 *K125 [131, 137, 143, 149], p1, k5, p1; rep from * once more.

Round 8 As round 7.

Round 9 *K1 [0, 1, 0, 1], (p3, k1) 31 [32, 34, 35, 37] times, p0 [3, 0, 3, 0], p1, k1, m1, k3, m1, k1, p1; rep from * once more.

Round 10 *K125 [131, 137, 143, 149], p1, k7, p1; rep from * once more.

Round 11 As round 10.

Round 12 *P2 [1, 2, 1, 2], k1, (p3, k1) 30 [32, 33, 35, 36] times, p3 [2, 3, 2, 3], k7, p1; rep from * once more.

Cont in this way, keeping cont of patt and inc 1 st inside border of 1 st at each end of each gusset on next round and 3 foll 4th rounds. Work 1 round.

Next round *P126 [132, 138, 144, 150], k15, p1; rep from * once more.

Rep last round once.

Next round *P126 [132, 138, 144, 150], k1, m1, k13, m1, p1; rep from * once more.

Next round *K125 [131, 137, 143, 149], p1, k17, p1; rep from * once more.

Rep last round twice.

Next round *P126 [132, 138, 144, 150], k1, m1, k15, m1, k1, p1; rep from * once more.

Next round *P126 [132, 138, 144, 150], k19, p1; rep from * once more.

Rep last round once more.

Next round *K125 [131, 137, 143, 149], p1, k19, p1; rep from * once more.

Next round *K125 [131, 137, 143, 149], p1, k1, m1, k17, m1, k1, p1; rep from * once more.

Next round *P1, (k1, p1) 62 [65, 68, 71, 74] times, p1, k21, p1; rep from * once more.

Next round *K125 [131, 137, 143, 149], p1, k21, p1; rep from * once more.

Rep last round once.

Next round *K1 (p1, k1) 62 [65, 68, 71, 74] times , p1, k21, p1; rep from * once more.

Next round *K125 [131, 137, 143, 149], p1, k21, p1; rep from * once more.

Divide for back and front

Next row K125 [131, 137, 143, 149] sts and turn; leave rem sts on a spare needle.

Complete back first.

***Work backwards and forwards as follows:

Row 1 (Wrong side) K1, (p1, k1) to end.

Row 2 Knit.

Row 3 Purl.

Row 4 As row 1.

Row 5 Purl.

Row 6 Knit.

Rep these 6 rows 2 [3, 3, 4, 4] times.

K 1 row. P 1 row. K 2 rows. P 1 row. K 2 rows. P 1 row. K 1 row.

Row 1 Knit.

Row 2 Purl.

Row 3 K1 [0, 1, 0, 1], (p3, k1) to last 0 [3, 0, 3, 0] sts, p0 [3, 0, 3, 0].

Row 4 Purl.

Row 5 Knit.

Row 6 K2 [1, 2, 1, 2], (p1, k3) to last 3 [2, 3, 2, 3] sts, p1, k2 [1, 2, 1, 2].

Rep these 6 rows 3 times.

K 1 row. P 2 rows. K 1 row. P 1 row.

Shape neck

Next row P46 [48, 50, 52, 54], cast off 33 [35, 37, 39, 41], p to end.

Complete right shoulder first.

Next row K to last 2 sts, k2 tog.

Next row Purl.

Next row P to last 2 sts, p2 tog.

Next row Knit.

Next row P to last 2 sts, p2 tog.

Next row Purl.

Next row K to last 2 sts, k2 tog.

P 2 rows. K 1 row. P 2 rows. K 1 row. Leave rem 42 [44, 46, 48, 50] sts on a stitch holder.*** With right side of back facing, rejoin yarn to rem sts, k2 tog, k to end.

Next row Purl.

Next row P2 tog, p to end.

Next row Knit.

Next row P2 tog, p to end.

Next row Purl.

Next row K2 tog, k to end.

P 2 rows. K 1 row. P 2 rows. K 1 row. Leave rem 42 [44, 46, 48, 50] sts on a stitch holder.

With right side of front facing, sl 23 sts on to a safety pin, rejoin yarn to rem sts, k to last 23 sts and sl these sts on to a safety pin. Work as given for back from *** to *** but leave sts on needle.

Join shoulders

With back and front right sides together, cast off 42 [44, 46, 48, 50] sts taking 1 st from each needle and working into them tog. Work other shoulder in same way.

NECKBAND

With right side facing, using circular needle size 3.75mm and beg 5 rows down from left back shoulder, pick up and k 4 sts to shoulder, 10 sts down left front neck, 33 [35, 37, 39, 41] sts from centre front, 10 sts up right front neck, 10 sts down right back neck, 33 [35, 37, 39, 41] sts from centre back and 6 sts up left back neck, then cast on 4 sts. *110 [114, 118, 122, 126] sts.* Work backwards and forwards as follows:

Row 1 (Wrong side) K6, (p2, k2) to last 4 sts, k4.

Row 2 K4, (p2, k2) to last 6 sts, p2, k4.

Row 3 As row 1.

Row 4 K2, yfwd, k2 tog, rib to last 4 sts, k4.

Rep rows 1 and 2 twice, then work rows 3 and 4. Work 1 row. Cast off in rib. Overlap the first 4 sts over the cast-on sts and catch down the cast-on sts to wrong side. Sew on buttons.

SLEEVES

With right side facing and using set of double-pointed needles size 3.75mm, pick up and k 88 [96, 96, 104, 104] sts evenly around armhole then p1, k21, p1 from safety pin. Work in rounds as follows:

Next round P89 [97, 97, 105, 105], k21, p1.

Rep last round once.

Next round P89 [97, 97, 105, 105], skpo, k17, k2 tog, p1.

Commence patt.

Round 1 K88 [96, 96, 104, 104], p1, k19, p1.

Round 2 (P1, k1) to last 21 sts, p1, k19, p1.

Round 3 As round 1.

Round 4 (K1, p1) to last 21 sts, p1, skpo, k15, k2 tog, p1.

These 4 rounds establish patt.

Next round Patt 88 [96, 96, 104, 104], p1, k17, p1.

Rep last round twice.

Next round Patt 88 [96, 96, 104, 104], p1, skpo, k13, k2 tog, p1.

Next round Patt 88 [96, 96, 104, 104], p1, k15, p1.

Rep last round twice.

Cont in this way, keeping cont of patt and dec 1 st inside border of 1 st at each end of gusset on next round and 3 foll 4th rounds. Work 3 rounds.

Next round P89 [97, 97, 105, 105], skpo, k3, k2 tog, p1.
Next round P89 [97, 97, 105, 105], k5, p1.
Rep last round once.
Next round K88 [96, 96, 104, 104], p1, k5, p1.
Next round K88 [96, 96, 104, 104], p1, skpo, k1, k2 tog, p1.
Next round K88 [96, 96, 104, 104], p1, k3, p1.
Next round P89 [97, 97, 105, 105], k3, p1.
Rep last round once.
Next round P89 [97, 97, 105, 105], sl 1,

k2 tog, psso, p1.
Cont in st st as follows:
Next round K88 [96, 96, 104, 104], p3.
Next round K88 [96, 96, 104, 104], p1, k1, p1.
Work 2 rounds.
Next round Skpo, k84 [92, 92, 100, 100], k2 tog, p3.
Cont in this way, dec 1 st at beg and end of st st part on every foll 11th [9th, 10th, 7th, 8th] round until 73 [75, 77, 79, 81] sts rem.
Cont straight until sleeve measures 40 [41, 41,

41, 42]cm from beg.
Next round K6 [5, 5, 7, 7], *k2 tog, k6 [10, 7, 10, 7]; rep from * 6 [4, 6, 4, 6] times more, k2 tog, k6 [5, 4, 7, 6], p2 tog, p1.
64 [68, 68, 72, 72] sts.
Work 6 [6, 7, 8, 8]cm in rounds of k2, p2 rib.
Cast off in rib.

FINISHING

Block as given on page 139.

Sanquhar Gansey

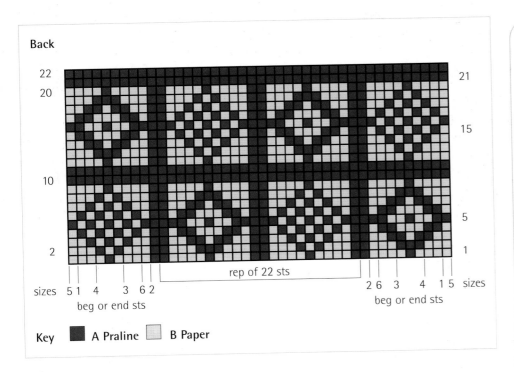

Back

22
20
10
2

21
15
5
1

rep of 22 sts

sizes 5 1 4 3 6 2
beg or end sts

2 6 3 4 1 5 sizes
beg or end sts

Key ■ A Praline □ B Paper

❋ MATERIALS
Yarn
Rowan Pure Wool Aran (approx
170m/186 yards)
A 5 [5, 6, 6, 7, 7] x 100g balls, shade 677
Praline
B 4 [5, 5, 6, 6, 7] x 100g balls, shade 671
Paper
Needles
1 pair size 4mm
1 pair size 4.5mm
1 set of four double-pointed needles size
4.5mm
Notions
2 stitch holders

❋ MEASUREMENTS
To fit chest 86 [91, 97, 102, 107, 112]cm
34 [36, 38, 40, 42, 44]in
Actual chest size 104 [110, 116, 122, 128,
134]cm
41, 43¼, 45¾, 48, 50½, 52¾]in
Length to back neck 62 [62, 62, 66, 66,
66]cm
24½ [24½, 24½, 26, 26, 26]in
Sleeve seam 45 [45, 46, 49, 49, 50]cm
17½ [17½, 18, 19¼, 19¼, 19¾]in
Tension
20 sts and 22 rows measure 10cm over
pattern on 4.5mm needles (or size
needed to obtain given tension)

BACK

Using 4mm needles and yarn A, cast on 96
[100, 108, 112, 120, 124] sts.
Carry yarn not in use loosely across wrong
side of work. Cont as follows:
Row 1 (Right side) (K2B, p2A) to end.
Row 2 (K2A, p2B) to end.
Rep these 2 rows until rib measures 6cm,
ending with row 2. Change to 4.5mm needles.
Next row Using yarn A, k7 [6, 9, 6, 6, 7], *inc
in next st, k8 [7, 9, 8, 11, 9]; rep from * to last
8 [6, 9, 7, 6, 7] sts, inc in next st, k to end.
106 [112, 118, 124, 130, 136] sts.
P1 row in yarn A. Beg with a k row, cont in
st st and patt from chart for back, working
odd-numbered (k) rows from right to left
and even-numbered (p) rows from left to
right until work measures approximately
62 [62, 62, 66, 66, 66]cm from beg, ending
with row 10 [10, 10, 22, 22, 22]. Leave these
sts on a spare needle.

FRONT

Work as given for back, until front measures
12 rows less than back.
Shape neck
Next row Patt 44 [46, 48, 50, 52, 54] sts and
turn; leave rem sts on a spare needle.
Complete left side of neck first. Cast off 3 sts
at beg of next row and foll alt row and 2 sts
at beg of foll 2 alt rows. Patt 4 rows straight.
34 [36, 38, 40, 42, 44] sts.
Join left shoulder
With back and front wrong sides together and
using yarn A, cast off 34 [36, 38, 40, 42, 44]
sts taking 1 st from each needle and working
them tog. Sl next 38 [40, 42, 44, 46, 48] sts on
back on to a stitch holder. With right side of
front facing, sl centre 18 [20, 22, 24, 26, 28]
sts on to a stitch holder, rejoin yarns to rem
sts and patt to end. Patt 1 row. Cast off 3 sts
at beg of next row and foll alt row and 2 sts
at beg of foll 2 alt rows. Patt 3 rows straight.
34 [36, 38, 40, 42, 44] sts.

Join right shoulder
Work as given for left shoulder.

SLEEVES

Using 4mm needles and yarn A, cast on
44 [44, 48, 48, 52, 52] sts. Work 6cm in rib
as given for back welt, ending with row 2.
Change to 4.5mm needles.
Next row Using yarn A, k4 [4, 4, 6, 5, 5], *inc
in next st, k2 [2, 4, 1, 2, 2]; rep from * to last

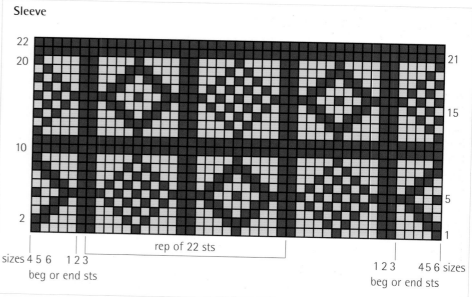

Sleeve

rep of 22 sts

sizes 4 5 6 1 2 3
beg or end sts

1 2 3   4 5 6 sizes
beg or end sts

4 [4, 4, 6, 5, 5] sts, inc in next st, k to end. *57 [57, 57, 67, 67, 67] sts.*
P 1 row in A. Beg with a k row, cont in st st and patt, working from chart for sleeve, inc 1 st at each end of every 7th [6th, 5th, 7th, 6th, 5th] row until there are 75 [79, 83, 87, 91, 95] sts, working extra sts into patt. Patt 13 [10, 11, 17, 15, 19] rows straight.

1st, 2nd and 3rd sizes
Next row Using yarn A, k4 [6, 8], (inc in st, k10) to last 5 [7, 9] sts, inc in next st, k to end. *82 [86, 90] sts.*
Next row P2 [0, 2] B, (k2A, p2B) to last 0 [2, 0] sts, k0 [2, 0] A.
Next row P0 [2, 0] A, (k2B, p2A) to last 2 [0, 2] sts, k2 [0, 2] B.

4th, 5th and 5th sizes
Next row Using yarn A, p [10, 12, 14], (inc in next st, p10) to last [11, 13, 15] sts, inc in next st, p to end. *[94, 98, 102] sts.*
Next row P [2, 0, 2] A, (k2B, p2A) to last [0, 2, 0] sts, k [0, 2, 0] B.
Next row P [0, 2, 0] B, (k2A, p2B) to last [2, 0, 2] sts, k [2, 0, 2] A.
All sizes
Rep last 2 rows until sleeve measures 45 [45, 46, 49, 50]cm from beg, ending with a wrong-side row. Using yarn A, cast off in rib.

NECKBAND

With right side of work facing, using double-pointed needles and yarn A, pick up and k 16 sts down left front neck, k18 [20, 22, 24, 26, 28] centre front sts, pick up and k 16 sts up right front neck, k38 [40, 42, 44, 48, 48] centre back sts. *88 [92, 96, 100, 104, 108] sts.* Divide sts on to three needles. Work 5 rounds of k2B, p2A rib. Using yarn A, rib 1 round. Cast off in rib.

FINISHING

Block each piece as given on page 139. Mark positions of armholes 21 [22, 23, 24, 25, 26]cm down from shoulders on back and front. Sew in sleeves. Join side and sleeve seams.

Eriskay Gansey

Part of body panel A
Plain Diamond

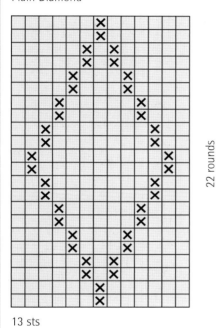

13 sts

22 rounds

Part of body panel A
Double Moss Stitch Diamond

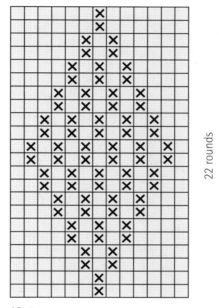

13 sts

22 rounds

❊ MATERIALS
Yarn
9 [10] x 100g balls Wendy (Poppleton's)
5-ply Guernsey wool (100% worsted wool,
approx 224m/245 yards) shade Cream
Needles
1 circular needle size 2.75mm, 80cm long
Set of four double-pointed needles size
2.75mm
1 cable needle
Notions
2 [3] buttons, 1.5cm in diameter
2 stitch holders
Special abbreviation
bind 1(2)(3) yfwd, knit 1(2)(3), pass
yfwd over knit 1(2)(3)

❊ MEASUREMENTS
Traditionally these ganseys are worn
close-fitting
To fit chest 81–91 [97–102]cm
32–36 [38–40]in
Actual chest size 92 [102]cm 36¼ [40¼]in
Length to back neck 65 [67]cm
25 [26½]in
Sleeve seam 47 [55]cm
18½ [21¾]in
Tension
28 sts and 37 rows measure 10cm over
body pattern on 2.75mm needles (or size
needed to obtain given tension)

BODY PANEL A

Double Moss Stitch and Plain Diamonds
Repeat of 11 [13] sts
Rounds 1 and 2 K5 [6], p1, k5 [6].
Rounds 3 and 4 K4 [5], p1, k1, p1, k4 [5].
Rounds 5 and 6 K3 [4], (p1, k1) twice, p1, k3 [4].
Rounds 7 and 8 K2 [3], (p1, k1) 3 times, p1, k2 [3].
Rounds 9 and 10 K1 [2], (p1, k1) 4 times, p1, k1 [2].
2nd size only
Rounds 11 and 12 K1, (p1, k1) 6 times.
Rounds 13 and 14 K2, (p1, k1) 4 times, p1, k2.
Both sizes
Rounds 11 [15] and 12 [16] As rounds 7 and 8.
Rounds 13 [17] and 14 [18] As rounds 5 and 6.
Rounds 15 [19] and 16 [20] As rounds 3 and 4.
Rounds 17 [21] and 18 [22] As rounds 1 and 2.

1st size only
Round 19 (Bind 2) twice, yfwd, k3, pass yfwd over k3, (bind 2) twice.
2nd size only
Round 23 (Bind 2) 3 times, k1, (bind 2) 3 times.
Both sizes
Round 20 [24] Knit.
Rounds 21 [25] and 22 [26] As rounds 19 [23] and 20 [24].
Rounds 23 [27]–26 [30] As rounds 1–4.
Rounds 27 [31] and 28 [32] K3 [4], p1, k3, p1, k3 [4].
Rounds 29 [33] and 30 [34] K2 [3], p1, k5, p1, k2 [3].
Rounds 31 [35] and 32 [36] K1 [2], p1, k7, p1, k1 [2].
2nd size only
Rounds 37 and 38 K1, p1, k9, p1, k1.
Rounds 39 and 40 K2, p1, k7, p1, k2.

Both sizes
Rounds 33 [41] and 34 [42] As rounds 29 [33] and 30 [34].
Rounds 35 [43] and 36 [44] As rounds 27 [31] and 28 [32].
Rounds 37 [45] and 38 [46] As rounds 3 and 4.
Rounds 39 [47] and 40 [48] As rounds 1 and 2.
Rounds 41 [49]–44 [52] As rounds 19 [23]–22 [26].
These 44 [52] rounds form panel A.

Body panel B Marriage Lines

13 rounds

13 sts

BODY PANEL B

Marriage Lines
Repeat of 11 [13] sts
Round 1 K1, p1, k9 [11].
Round 2 K1, p2, k8 [10].
Round 3 K2, p2, k7 [9].
Round 4 K3, p2, k6 [8].
Round 5 K4, p2, k5 [7].
Round 6 K5, p2, k4 [6].
Round 7 K6, p2, k3 [5].
Round 8 K7, p2, k2 [4].
Round 9 K8, p2, k1 [3].
2nd size only
Round 10 K9, p2, k2.
Round 11 K10, p2, k1.
Both sizes
Round 10 [12] K9 [11], p1, k1.
Round 11 [13] Knit.
These 11 [13] rounds form panel B.

BODY PANEL C

Wave
Repeat of 11 [13] sts
Rounds 1 and 2 (K1, p1) twice, k7 [9].
Rounds 3 and 4 K2, p1, k1, p1, k6 [8].
Rounds 5 and 6 K3, p1, k1, p1, k5 [7].
Rounds 7 and 8 K4, p1, k1, p1, k4 [6].
Rounds 9 and 10 K5, p1, k1, p1, k3 [5].
Rounds 11 and 12 K6, p1, k1, p1, k2 [4].
Rounds 13 and 14 K7, p1, k1, p1, k1 [3].
2nd size only
Rounds 15 and 16 K8, p1, k1, p1, k2.

Body panel C Wave

32 rounds

13 sts

Rounds 17 and 18 K9, (p1, k1) twice.
Rounds 19 and 20 As rounds 15 and 16.
Rounds 21 and 22 As rounds 13 and 14.
Both sizes
Rounds 15 [23] and 16 [24] As rounds 11 and 12.
Rounds 17 [25] and 18 [26] As rounds 9 and 10.
Rounds 19 [27] and 20 [28] As rounds 7 and 8.
Rounds 21 [29] and 22 [30] As rounds 5 and 6.
Rounds 23 [31] and 24 [32] As rounds 3 and 4.
These 24 [32] rounds form panel C.

BODY PANEL D

Small Starfish and Diamond
Repeat of 13 sts
Round 1 K1, p1, k9, p1, k1.
Round 2 K1, p2, k7, p2, k1.
Round 3 K2, p2, k5, p2, k2.
Round 4 K3, (p2, k3) twice.

Body panel D Small Starfish and Diamond

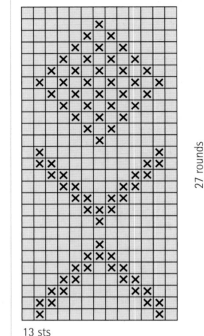

27 rounds

13 sts

Round 5 K4, p2, k1, p2, k4.
Round 6 K5, p3, k5.
Round 7 K6, p1, k6.
Round 8 Knit.
Round 9 As round 7.
Round 10 As round 6.
Round 11 As round 5.
Round 12 As round 4.
Round 13 As round 3.
Round 14 As round 2.
Round 15 As round 1.
Round 16 As round 7.
Round 17 K5, p1, k1, p1, k5.
Round 18 K4, (p1, k1) twice, p1, k4.
Round 19 K3, (p1, k1) 3 times, p1, k3.
Round 20 K2, (p1, k1) 4 times, p1, k2.
Round 21 K1, (p1, k1) 6 times.
Round 22 As round 20.
Round 23 As round 19.
Round 24 As round 18.
Round 25 As round 17.
Round 26 As round 7.
Round 27 Knit.
These 27 rounds form panel D.

YOKE PANEL E

Tree of Life, Anchor, Open Diamond
Repeat of 17 sts
Row 1 (Right side) K7, p1, k1, p1, k7.
Row 2 P6, k2, p1, k2, p6.
Row 3 K5, p2, k3, p2, k5.
Row 4 P4, k2, p5, k2, p4.
Row 5 K3, p2, k2, p1, k1, p1, k2, p2, k3.
Row 6 (P2, k2) twice, p1, (k2, p2) twice.
Row 7 K1, p2, k2, p2, k3, p2, k2, p2, k1.
Row 8 P1, k1, p2, k2, p5, k2, p2, k1, p1.
Rows 9 and 10 As rows 5 and 6.
Row 11 K2, p1, k2, p2, k3, p2, k2, p1, k2.
Rows 12 and 13 As rows 4 and 5.
Row 14 P3, k1, p2, k2, p1, k2, p2, k1, p3.
Rows 15 and 16 As rows 3 and 4.
Row 17 K4, p1, k2, p1, k1, p1, k2, p1, k4.
Rows 18 and 19 As rows 2 and 3.
Row 20 P5, (k1, p5) twice.
Rows 21 and 22 As rows 1 and 2.
Row 23 K6, p1, k3, p1, k6.
Row 24 Purl.
Row 25 As row 1.
Row 26 P7, k1, p1, k1, p7.
Row 27 (Bind 2) 4 times, bind 1, (bind 2) 4 times.
Row 28 Purl.
Rows 29 and 30 As rows 27 and 28.
Row 31 K8, p1, k8.
Row 32 P7, k3, p7.
Row 33 K6, p5, k6.
Row 34 P5, k2, p1, k1, p1, k2, p5.
Row 35 K4, p2, k2, p1, k2, p2, k4.
Row 36 P3, k2, p3, k1, p3, k2, p3.
Row 37 K2, p2, k4, p1, k4, p2, k2.
Row 38 P1, k2, p5, k1, p5, k2, p1.
Row 39 K1, p1, (k6, p1) twice, k1.
Row 40 P2, k1, p5, k1, p8.
Row 41 K8, p1, k4, p2, k2.
Row 42 P3, k2, p3, k1, p8.
Row 43 K8, p1, k2, p2, k4.
Row 44 P5, k2, p1, k1, p8.
Row 45 K8, p3, k6.
Row 46 P7, k2, p8.
Row 47 K7, p2, k8.
Row 48 P8, k3, p6.
Row 49 K5, p2, k1, p1, k8.
Row 50 P8, k1, p2, k2, p4.
Row 51 K3, p2, k3, p1, k8.
Row 52 P8, k1, p4, k2, p2.

Row 53 K1, p2, k5, p1, k8.
Row 54 P8, k1, p6, k1, p1.
Row 55 K6, p5, k6.
Row 56 P6, k5, p6.
Row 57–60 As rows 27–30.
Row 61 K6, k2 tog, yfwd, k1, yfwd, skpo, k6.
Row 62 and every foll alt row Purl.
Row 63 K5, k2 tog, yfwd, k3, yfwd, skpo, k5.
Row 65 K4, (k2 tog, yfwd) twice, k1, (yfwd, skpo) twice, k4.
Row 67 K3, (k2 tog, yfwd) twice, k3, (yfwd, skpo) twice, k3.
Row 69 K2, (k2 tog, yfwd) twice, k5, (yfwd, skpo) twice, k2.
Row 71 K4, (yfwd, skpo) twice, k1, (k2 tog, yfwd) twice, k4.
Row 73 K5, yfwd, skpo, yfwd, sl 1, k2 tog, psso, yfwd, k2 tog, yfwd, k5.
Row 75 K6, yfwd, skpo, k1, k2 tog, yfwd, k6.
Row 77 K7, yfwd, sl 1, k2 tog, psso, yfwd, k7.
Row 78 Purl.
These 78 rows form panel E.

Note The Open Diamond, Horseshoe, Cable and Open Tree panel patterns are given only as line-by-line instructions.

Part of yoke panel E Tree of Life

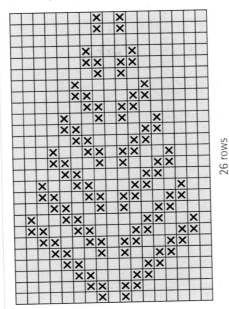

26 rows

17 sts

Part of yoke panel E Anchor

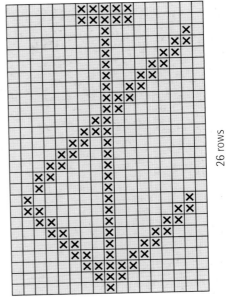

26 rows

17 sts

YOKE PANEL F

Horseshoe
Repeat of 9 [11] sts
2nd size only
Row 1 K1, yfwd, k3, sl 1, k2 tog, psso, k3, yfwd, k1.
Row 2 Purl
Both sizes
Row 1 [3] (Right side) K1 [2], yfwd, k2, sl 1, k2 tog, psso, k2, yfwd, k1 [2].
Row 2 [4] and foll alt row Purl.
Row 3 [5] K2 [3], yfwd, k1, sl 1, k2 tog, psso, k1, yfwd, k2 [3].
Row 5 [7] K3 [4], yfwd, sl 1, k2 tog, psso, yfwd, k3 [4].
Row 6 [8] Purl.
These 6 [8] rows form panel F.

YOKE PANEL G

Cable
Repeat of 6 [8] sts
Row 1 (Right side) K6 [8].
Row 2 P6 [8].
Rows 3–4 [6] Rep rows 1 and 2 once [twice].

Row 5 [7] Sl next 3 [4] sts onto cable needle and leave at back, k3 [4], k3 [4] sts from cable needle.
Row 6 [8] As row 2.
These 6 [8] rows form panel G.

YOKE PANEL H

Starfish, Open Tree, Diamond
Repeat of 17 sts
Row 1 (Right side) K4, p1, k7, p1, k4.

Part of yoke panel H Starfish

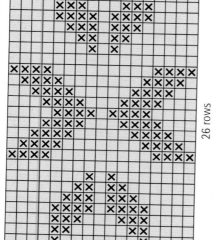

17 sts

Part of yoke panel H Diamond

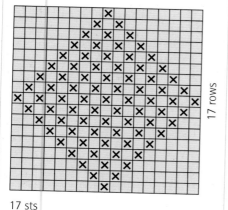

17 sts

Row 2 P4, k2, p5, k2, p4.
Row 3 K4, p3, k3, p3, k4.
Row 4 P4, k4, p1, k4, p4.
Row 5 K5, p3, k1, p3, k5.
Row 6 P6, k2, p1, k2, p6.
Row 7 K7, p1, k1, p1, k7.
Row 8 Purl.
Row 9 P4, k9, p4.
Row 10 P1, k4, p7, k4, p1.
Row 11 K2, p4, k5, p4, k2.
Row 12 P3, (k4, p3) twice.
Row 13 K4, p4, k1, p4, k4.
Row 14 As row 12.
Row 15 As row 11.
Row 16 As row 10.
Row 17 As row 9.
Row 18 Purl.
Row 19 As row 7.
Row 20 As row 6.
Row 21 As row 5.
Row 22 As row 4.
Row 23 As row 3.
Row 24 As row 2.
Row 25 As row 1.
Row 26 Purl.
Row 27 (Bind 2) 4 times, bind 1, (bind 2) 4 times.
Row 28 Purl.
Rows 29 and 30 As rows 27 and 28.
Row 31 K6, k2 tog, yfwd, k1, yfwd, skpo, k6.
Row 32 and 11 foll alt rows Purl.
Row 33 K5, k2 tog, yfwd, k3, yfwd, skpo, k5.
Row 35 K4, (k2 tog, yfwd) twice, k1, (yfwd, skpo) twice, k4.
Row 37 K3, (k2 tog, yfwd) twice, k3, (yfwd, skpo) twice, k3.
Row 39 K2, (k2 tog, yfwd) 3 times, k1, (yfwd, skpo) 3 times, k2.
Row 41 K1, (k2 tog, yfwd) 3 times, k3, (yfwd, skpo) 3 times, k1.
Row 43 (K2 tog, yfwd) 4 times, k1, (yfwd, skpo) 4 times.
Row 45 As row 41.
Row 47 As row 39.
Row 49 As row 37.
Row 51 As row 35.
Row 53 As row 33.
Row 55 As row 31.
Row 56 Purl.
Rows 57–60 As rows 27–30.
Row 61 K8, p1, k8.

Row 62 P7, k1, p1, k1, p7.
Row 63 K6, (p1, k1) twice, p1, k6.
Row 64 P5, (k1, p1) 3 times, k1, p5.
Row 65 K4, (p1, k1) 4 times, p1, k4.
Row 66 P3, (k1, p1) 5 times, k1, p3.
Row 67 K2, (p1, k1) 6 times, p1, k2.
Row 68 P1, (k1, p1) 8 times.
Rows 69 and 70 Rep row 68 twice.
Row 71 As row 67.
Row 72 As row 66.
Row 73 As row 65.
Row 74 As row 64.
Row 75 As row 63.
Row 76 As row 62.
Row 77 As row 61.
Row 78 Purl.
These 78 rows form panel H.

BACK AND FRONT

This garment is knitted in one piece up to the armholes. Using circular needle size 2.75mm, cast on 256 [280] sts. Work in rounds as follows:
Round 1 (P1, k1 tbl) to end.
Rep this round 13 times more.
Next round **K31 [23], *inc in next st, k63 [45]; rep from * 0 [1] times more, inc in next st, k32 [24]; rep from ** once more. *260 [286] sts.*
Next round (Bind 2) to end.
Next round Knit.
Rep last 2 rounds once more. Commence patt.
Round 1 *P1 [0], k1 [0], p1, work 11 [13] sts as round 1 of panel A, p1, k1, p1, work 11 [13] sts as round 1 of panel B, p1, k1, p1, work 11 [13] sts as round 1 of panel C, p1, k1, p1, work 11 [13] sts as round 1 of panel A, p1, k1, p1, work 13 sts as round 1 of panel D, p1, k1, p1, work 11 [13] sts as round 1 of panel A, p1, k1, p1, work 11 [13] sts as round 1 of panel C, p1, k1, p1, work 11 [13] sts as round 1 of panel B, p1, k1, p1, work 11 [13] sts as round 1 of panel A, p1, k1 [0]; rep from * once more.
Round 2 *P1 [0], k1 [0], p1, work 11 [13] sts as round 2 of panel A, p3, work 11 [13] sts as round 2 of panel B, p3, work 11 [13] sts as round 2 of panel C, p3, work 11 [13] sts as round 2 of panel A, p3, work 13 sts as round 2 of panel D, p3, work 11 [13] sts as round 2 of panel A, p3, work 11 [13] sts as round 2 of panel C, p3, work 11 [13] sts as round 2 of

panel B, p3, work 11 [13] sts as round 2 of panel A, p1, k1 [0]; rep from * once more. These 2 rounds establish patt for body. Cont in patt as set working appropriate rounds of panels until 126 [125] rounds in all have been worked.

Shape for gusset
2nd size only
Next round *Pick up loop lying between sts and p tbl, (k1, p1) all in next st, patt 141, (p1, k1) all in next st; rep from * once more.

Both sizes
Next round *P1, k1, p1, (bind 2) 61 [69] times, bind 3, p1, k1; rep from * once more.
Next round *P1, k1, p1, k125 [141], p1, k1; rep from *once more.
Next round *P1, k twice in next st, p1, (bind 2) 61 [69] times, bind 3, p1, k twice in next st; rep from * once more.
Next round *P1, k2, p1, k125 [141], p1, k2; rep from * once more.
Next round *P1, k twice in next st, k1, p1, k2,

(p1, k7) 15 [17] times, p1, k2, p1, k twice in next st, k1; rep from * once more.
Next round *P1, k3, p1, k3, (p1, k5, p1, k1) 15 [17] times, k2, p1, k3; rep from * once more.
Next round *P1, k3, p1, k3, (p1, k5, p1, k1) 15 [17] times, k2, p1, k3; rep from * once more.
Next round *P1, k1, k twice in next st, k1, p1, k4, (p1, k3) 30 [34] times, k1, p1, k twice in next st, k2; rep from * once more.
Next round *P1, k4, p1, k5, (p1, k1, p1, k5) 15 [17] times, p1, k4; rep from * once more.
Next round *P1, k2, k twice in next st, k1, p1, k6, (p1, k7) 14 [16] times, p1, k6, p1, k twice in next st, k3; rep from * once more.
Next round *P1, k5, p1, k5, (p1, k1, p1, k5) 15 [17] times, p1, k5; rep from * once more.
Next round *P1, k3, k twice in next st, k1, p1, k4, (p1, k3) 30 [34] times, k1, p1, k twice in next st, k4; rep from * once more.
Next round *P1, k6, p1, k3, (p1, k5, p1, k1) 15 [17] times, k2, p1, k6; rep from * once more.
Next round *P1, k4, k twice in next st, k1, p1, k2, (p1, k7) 15 [17] times, p1, k2, p1, k twice in next st, k5; rep from * once more.

2nd size only
Next round *P1, k7, p1, k3, (p1, k5, p1, k1) 17 times, k2, p1, k7; rep from * once more.

Next round *P1, k5, k twice in next st, k1, p1, k4, (p1, k3) 34 times, k1, p1, k twice in next st, k6; rep from * once more.
Next round *P1, k8, p1, k5, (p1, k1, p1, k5) 17 times, p1, k8; rep from * once more.
Next round *P1, k8, p1, k6, (p1, k7) 16 times, p1, k6, p1, k8; rep from * once more.
Next round *P1, k8, p1, k5, (p1, k1, p1, k5) 17 times, p1, k8; rep from * once more.
Next round *P1, k8, p1, k4 (p1, k3) 34 times, k1, p1, k8; rep from * once more.
Next round *P1, k8, p1, k3, (p1, k5, p1, k1) 17 times, k2, p1, k8; rep from * once more.
Next round *P1, k8, p1, k2, (p1, k7) 17 times, p1, k2, p1, k8; rep from * once more.
284 [320] sts.

Both sizes
Next round *P1, k7 [8], p1, (bind 2) 61 [69] times, bind 3, p1, k7 [8]; rep from * once more.
Next round **P1, k7 [8], p1, k9 [10], *inc in next st, k14 [16]; rep from * 6 times more, inc in next st, k10 [11], p1, k7 [8]; rep from ** once more.
300 [336] sts.

Divide for front
Next round *P1, k7 [8], p1 and sl these 9 [10] sts on to safety pin, (bind 2) 65 [73] times, bind 3, sl next 8 [9] sts on to safety pin and turn; leave rem sts on needle. Complete front first. Work backwards and forwards.
P 1 row. ***Commence yoke patt.
Row 1 K2, p9, k2 [3], p1, work 17 sts as row 1 of panel E, p1, k2 [3], p1, work 9 [11] sts as row 1 of panel F, p1, k2 [3], p1, work 6 [8] sts as row 1 of panel G, p1, k2 [3], p1, work 17 sts as row 1 of panel H, p1, k2 [3], p1, work 6 [8] sts as row 1 of panel G, p1, k2 [3], p1, work 9 [11] sts as row 1 of panel F, p1, k2 [3], p1, work 17 sts as row 1 of panel E, p1, k2 [3], p9, k2.
Row 2 P2, k9, p2 [3], k1, work 17 sts as row 2 of panel E, k1, p2 [3], k1, work 9 [11] sts as row 2 of panel F, k1, p2 [3], k1, work 6 [8] sts as row 2 of panel G, k1, p2 [3], k1, work 17 sts as row 2 of panel H, k1, p2 [3], k1, work 6 [8] sts as row 2 of panel G, k1, p2 [3], k1, work 9 [11] sts as row 2 of panel F, k1, p2 [3], k1, work 17 sts as row 2 of panel E, k1, p2 [3], k9, p2.
Row 3 K10, p1, bind 2 [3], p1, work 17 sts as row 3 of panel E, p1, bind 2 [3], p1, work 9 [11] sts as row 3 of panel F, p1, bind 2 [3], p1, work 6 [8] sts as row 3 of panel G, p1, bind 2

[3], p1, work 17 sts as row 3 panel H, p1, bind 2 [3], p1, work 6 [8] sts as row 3 of panel G, p1, bind 2 [3], p1, work 9 [11] sts as row 3 of panel F, p1, bind 2 [3], p1, work 17 sts as row 3 of panel E, p1, bind 2 [3], p1, k10.

Row 4 P10, k1, p2 [3], k1, work 17 sts as row 4 of panel E, k1, p2 [3], k1, work 9 [11] sts as row 4 of panel F, k1, p2 [3], k1, work 6 [8] sts as row 4 of panel G, k1, p2 [3], k1, work 17 sts as row 4 of panel H, k1, p2 [3], k1, work 6 [8] sts as row 4 of panel G, k1, p2 [3], k1, work 9 [11] sts as row 4 of panel F, k1, p2 [3], k1, work 17 sts as row 4 of panel E, k1, p2 [3], k1, p10.
These 4 rows establish patt for yoke. Cont in patt as set, working appropriate rows of panels until 78 rows in all have been worked***.

Shape neck

Next row K2, (bind 2) 20 [23] times, k2 and turn; leave rem sts on needle. Complete left front neck first.

Next row Purl.

Row 1 K2, (bind 2) to last 2 sts, k2.

Row 2 Purl.

Row 3 K2, (purl 1, k7) to last 2 [8] sts, p1, k1 [7].

Row 4 P2 [0], (k1, p5, k1, p1) to last 2 sts, p2.

Row 5 K4, (p1, k3) to last 4 [2] sts, p1, k3 [1].

Row 6 P4 [2], (k1, p1, k1, p5) to end.

Row 7 K6, (p1, k7) to last 6 [4] sts, p1, k5 [3]. Mark end of this row.

Row 8 As row 6.

Row 9 As row 5.

Row 10 As row 4.

Row 11 As row 3.

Row 12 Purl.

Rows 13–16 Rep rows 1 and 2 twice.
Leave these sts on a spare needle. With right side of front facing, sl centre 45 [49] sts on to a stitch holder, rejoin yarn to rem sts and k2, (bind 2) to last 2 sts, k2.

Next row Purl

Row 1 K2, (bind 2) to last 2 sts, k2.

Row 2 Purl.

Row 3 K1 [7], (p1, k7) to last 3 sts, p1, k2.

Row 4 P3, (k1, p5, k1, p1) to last 1 [7] sts, p1 [6], k0 [1].

Row 5 K3 [1], (p1, k3) to last st, k1.

Row 6 P5, k1, p1, k1) to last 4 [2] sts, p4 [2].

Row 7 K5 [3], (p1, k7) to last 7 sts, p1, k6.

Row 8 As row 6.

Row 9 As row 5.

Row 10 As row 4.

Row 11 As row 3.

Row 12 Purl.

Rows 13–16 Rep rows 1 and 2 twice.
Leave these sts on a spare needle. With right side of back facing, rejoin yarn to rem sts, p1, k7 [8], p1 and sl these 9 [10] sts on to a safety pin, (bind 2) 65 [73] times, bind 3, sl last 8 [9] sts on to a safety pin. P 1 row. Work as given for front from *** to ***.

Join shoulders With right sides of back and front together, cast off 44 [50] sts, taking 1 st from each needle and working them together, sl next 45 [49] centre back sts on to a stitch holder, rejoin yarn to rem sts and complete to match first shoulder.

NECKBAND

With right side facing, using circular needle size 2.75mm and beg at marker, pick up and k 7 sts down front neck, k 45 [49] centre front sts, pick up and k 10 sts up right front neck, k 45 [49] centre back sts, pick up and k 5 sts to marker and 2 sts behind the first 2 picked-up sts. *114 [122] sts.*
Work backwards and forwards as follows:

Row 1 (Wrong side) P2, k3, (p1 tbl, k1) to last 5 sts, k3, p2.

Row 2 K5, (p1, k1 tbl) to last 5 sts, k5.

Row 3 As row 1.

Row 4 K2, cast off 2, k1 (st used in casting off) (p1, k1 tbl) to last 5 sts, k5.

Row 5 P2, k3, (p1 tbl, k1) to last 3 sts, k1, cast on 2, p2.
Rep rows 2 and 3, 4 [3] times then rows 4 and 5 once.

2nd size only
Rep last 8 rows once more.

Both sizes
Rep rows 2 and 3 once. Cast off k-wise. Sew on buttons.

SLEEVES

With right side facing and using set of four double-pointed needles size 2.75mm, sl 9 [10] sts on safety pin on to needle, rejoin yarn and pick up and k 89 sts evenly around armhole edge, p1, k7 [8]. Work in rounds as follows:

Next round P1, k4 [5], k2 tog, k1, p91, k1, skpo, k4 [5].

Next round P1, k3 [4], k2 tog, k1, p91, k1, skpo, k3 [4].

1st size only

Next round P1, k2, k2 tog, k1, p1, k9, p2, work 11 sts as round 1 of panel B, p1, k1, p1, work 11 sts as round 1 of panel C, p1, k1, p1, work 11 sts as round 1 of panel A, p1, k1, p1, work 11 sts as round 1 of panel C, p1, k1, p1, work 11 sts as round 1 of panel B, p2, k9, p1, k1 skpo, k2.

Next round P1, k1, k2 tog, k1, p1, k9, p2, work 11 sts as round 2 of panel B, p3, work 11 sts as round 2 of panel C, p3, work 11 sts as round 2 of panel A, p3, work 11 sts as round 2 of panel C, p3, work 11 sts as round 2 of panel B, p2, k9, p1, k1, skpo, k1.
These 2 rounds establish patt.

2nd size only

Next round P1, k3, k2 tog, k1, p1, k19, p1, k1, p1, work 13 sts as round 1 of panel B, p1, k1, p1, work 13 sts as round 1 of panel A, p1, k1, p1, work 13 sts as round 1 of panel B, p1, k1, p1, k19, p1, k1, skpo, k3.

Next round P1, k2, k2 tog, k1, p1, k19, p3, work 13 sts as round 2 of panel B, p3, work 13 sts as round 2 of panel A, p3, work 13 sts as round 2 of panel B, p3, k19, p1, k1, skpo, k2.
These 2 rounds establish patt.

Next round P1, k1, k2 tog, k1, p1, patt to last 5 sts, p1, k1, skpo, k1.

Both sizes
Cont in patt as set, working appropriate rounds of panels, work as follows:

Next round P1, k1, k2 tog, p1, patt to last 4 sts, p1, skpo, k1.

Next round P1, k3, patt to last 3 sts, k3.
Rep last round 35 [39] times more.

Next round P1, k1, skpo, patt to last 3 sts, k2 tog, k1. Patt 6 [7] rounds straight. Rep last 7 [8] rounds 14 times more. *66 sts.*
Work a further 10 [18] rounds straight.

Next round (P1, k1 tbl) to end.
Rep last round 14 times more.
Cast off knitwise.

FINISHING

Block as given on page 139.

Caister Fisherman's Gansey

BACK AND FRONT

This garment is knitted in one piece to the armholes.

Back welt Using circular needle size 3mm, cast on 124 [132, 140, 148, 156, 164] sts. K 20 rows. Leave these sts on needle. Work front welt as back welt and turn.

Next round **P1, k8 [4, 8, 5, 9, 5], *inc in next st, k6 [7, 7, 8, 8, 9]; rep from * 14 times more, inc in next st, k8 [5, 9, 5, 9, 6], p1**; now work from ** to ** across back welt sts.
280 [296, 312, 328, 344, 360] sts.

Work in rounds as follows:

Round 1 *P1, k138 [146, 154, 162, 170, 178], p1; rep from * once more.

Rep last round until work measures 31 [32, 33, 34, 35, 36]cm from beg. Commence yoke patt.

Rounds 1 and 2 Purl.
Rounds 3 and 4 *P1, k138 [146, 154, 162, 170, 178], p1; rep from * once more.
Rounds 5–8 As rounds 1–4.
Rounds 9 and 10 As rounds 1 and 2.
Round 11 *P1, k33 [37, 41, 45, 49, 53], (m1, k2, m1, k6) 3 times, k30, (m1, k2, m1, k6) 3 times, k27 [31, 35, 39, 43, 47], p1; rep from * once more. *304 [320, 336, 352, 368, 384] sts.*
Round 12 *P3, (k2, p2) 7 [8, 9, 10, 11, 12] times,

k30, p2, (k2, p2) 7 times, k30, (p2, k2) 7 [8, 9, 10, 11, 12] times, p3; rep from * once more.
Round 13 *P1, k30 [34, 38, 42, 46, 50], (p2, k6, p2) 3 times, k30, (p2, k6, p2) 3 times, k30 [34, 38, 42, 46, 50], p1; rep from * once more.
Round 14 *P1, k2, (p2, k2) 7 [8, 9, 10, 11, 12] times, k32, (p2, k2) 7 times, k32, (p2, k2) 7 [8, 9, 10, 11, 12] times, p1; rep from * once more.
Round 15 As round 13.
Rounds 16–23 Rep rounds 12–15 twice.
Rounds 24 and 25 As rounds 12 and 13.
Round 26 *P1, k2, (p2, k2) 7 [8, 9, 10, 11, 12] times, (k2, c6b, k2) 3 times, k2, (p2, k2) 7 times, (k2, c6b, k2) 3 times, k2, (p2, k2) 7 [8, 9, 10, 11, 12] times, p1; rep from * once more.
Round 27 As round 13.
Rep rounds 12–27 once more.

Divide for front

Next row P1 and sl this st on to safety pin, m1, p2, (k2, p2) 7 [8, 9, 10, 11, 12] times, k30, p2, (k2, p2) 7 times, k30, (p2, k2) 7 [8, 9, 10, 11, 12] times, p2, m1 and turn; leave rem sts on needle.
***Work backwards and forwards.
Row 1 (Wrong side) K1, p30 [34, 38, 42, 46, 50], (k2, p6, k2) 3 times, p30, (k2, p6, k2) 3 times, p30 [34, 38, 42, 46, 50], k1.
Row 2 K3, (p2, k2) 7 [8, 9, 10, 11, 12] times, k32, (p2, k2) 7 times, k32, (p2, k2) 7 [8, 9, 10, 11, 12] times, k1.
Row 3 As row 1.
Row 4 K1, p2, (k2, p2) 7 [8, 9, 10, 11, 12] times, k30, p2, (k2, p2) 7 times, k30, (p2, k2) 7 [8, 9, 10, 11, 12] times, p2, k1.
Rows 5–12 Rep rows 1–4 twice.
Row 13 As row 1.
Row 14 K3, (p2, k2) 7 [8, 9, 10, 11, 12] times, (k2, c6b, k2) 3 times, k2 (p2, k2) 7 times, (k2, c6b, k3) 3 times, k2, (p2, k2) 7 [8, 9, 10, 11, 12] times, k1.
Row 15 As row 1.
Row 16 As row 4.
These 16 rows form patt. Cont in patt until armholes measure 17 [18, 19, 20, 21, 22]cm, ending with a wrong-side row.
Next row Patt 33 [37, 41, 45, 49, 53], (k2 tog, k1, k2 tog, k5) 3 times, patt 30, (k2 tog, k1,

❋ MATERIALS

Yarn

7 [7, 8, 9, 9, 10] x 100g balls Frangipani 5-ply Guernsey wool (100% wool, approx 225m/245 yards, shade Sea Spray (also available in 500g cones, approx 1130m/1240 yards)

Needles

1 circular needle size 3mm, 80cm long
1 set of four double-pointed needles size 3mm
1 cable needle

Notions

2 stitch holders

Special abbreviations

m1 Pick up loop lying between sts and k tbl

c6b Sl next 3 sts on to cable needle and leave at back of work, k3 from left-hand needle, k3 from cable needle

❋ MEASUREMENTS

To fit chest 87 [91, 97, 102, 107, 112]cm
34 [36, 38, 40, 42, 44]in
Actual chest size 100 [106, 111, 117, 122 128]cm
39¼ [41¾, 43¾, 46, 48, 50¼]in
Length to back neck 57 [59, 61, 63, 65, 67]cm
22½ [23, 24, 24¾, 25½, 26¼]in
Sleeve seam 43 [44, 45, 46, 47, 48]cm
17 [17¼, 17¾, 18, 18½, 19]in

Tension

28 sts and 36 rows measure 10cm over stocking stitch on 3mm needles (or size needed to obtain given tension)

k2 tog, k5) 3 times, patt 29 [33, 37, 41, 45, 49].
140 [148, 156, 164, 172, 180] sts***.
Next row K1, p to last st, k1.
Shape neck
Next row Patt 46 [49, 52, 55, 58, 61] sts and turn; leave rem sts on needle.
Complete left front neck first.

Chest bands and seed stitch

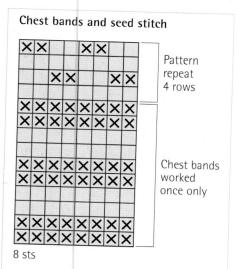

Pattern repeat 4 rows

Chest bands worked once only

8 sts

Round 10 As round 2.
Round 11 P2, (k2, p2) to end.
Round 12 As round 2.
Round 13 As round 9.
Round 14 As round 8.
Round 15 P1, k2, (p2, k2) to last st, p1.
Round 16 As round 2.
Round 17 Purl.
Next round P1, k to last st, p1.
Rep this round once more.
Next round P1, skpo, k to last 3 sts, k2 tog, p1.
Next round P1, k to last st, p1.
Rep last round 4 [3, 3, 2, 2, 2] times more.
Rep last 6 [5, 5, 4, 4, 4] rounds until 62 [62, 64, 64, 66, 68] sts rem, ending with dec round.
Cont straight until sleeve measures 36 [37, 38, 39, 40, 41]cm, ending 1 st before end of last round.
Next round P2 tog, k9 [9, 10, 10, 9, 8], *k2 tog, k8 [8, 8, 8, 9, 6]; rep from * to last 11 [11, 12, 12, 11, 10] sts, k2 tog, k to end.
56 [56, 58, 58, 60, 60] sts.
Work 7cm in rounds of k1, p1 rib. Cast off in rib.

FINISHING

Block as given on page 139.

Row 1 Purl.
Rows 2 and 3 Knit.
Row 4 Purl.
Rep these 4 rows 5 times more then rows 1 and 2 once. Leave these sts on spare needle.
With right side of front facing, sl centre 48 [50, 52, 54, 56, 58] sts on to stitch holder, rejoin yarn to rem sts and p to end. Complete to match left front neck.
With right side of back facing, rejoin yarn to rem sts, p1 and sl this st on to safety pin, m1, p2, (k2, p2) 7 [8, 9, 10, 11, 12] times, k30, p2, (k2, p2) 7 times, k30, (p2, k2) 7 [8, 9, 10, 11, 12] times, p2, m1. Work as given for front from *** to ***.

Join shoulders
With right sides of back and front together, cast off 46 [49, 52, 55, 58, 61] sts taking 1 st from each needle and working them tog. Sl next 48 [50, 52, 54, 56, 58] centre back sts on to stitch holder, rejoin yarn to rem sts and complete to match first shoulder.

NECKBAND

With right side facing and using set of four double-pointed needles size 3mm, pick up and k 18 sts down left front neck, k across 48 [50, 52, 54, 56, 58] centre front sts, pick up and k 18 sts up right front neck and k across 48 [50, 52, 54, 56, 58] centre back sts.

132 [136, 140, 144, 148, 152] sts.
Work 12 rounds in K1, p1, rib. Cast off in rib.

SLEEVES

With right side facing and using set of four double-pointed needles size 3mm, p1 from safety pin, pick up and k 108 [116, 120, 128, 132, 140] sts evenly around armhole edge then p1 from safety pin. Work in rounds as follows:
Round 1 P1, k to last st, p1.
Round 2 P1, skpo, k to last 3 sts, k2 tog, p1.
Rep last 2 rounds 4 times more. Commence band patt.
Round 1 Purl.
Round 2 P1, k to last st, p1.
Round 3 P3, (k2, p2) to last st, p1.
Round 4 As round 2.
Round 5 P1, (k2, p2) to last 3 sts, k2, p1.
Rounds 6 and 7 As rounds 2 and 3.
Round 8 P1, skpo, k to last 3 sts, k2 tog, p1.
Round 9 P1, k1, (p2, k2) to last 4 sts, p2, k1, p1.

Fair Isle

The Shetland Islands, which include tiny Fair Isle, have always been a thriving centre for traders and fishermen, as they have a large, safe harbour at Lerwick, sheltered by the island of Bressay. Many sea routes converged on Shetland over the centuries, and the harbour was a haven for hundreds of ships of all nationalities in their journey from the south of Europe to the Baltic, Scandina via, the Faroe Islands and Iceland.

It is difficult to ascertain the exact origins of Fair Isle patterns, but they seem to be related to patterns found in Estonia and Russia and could easily have been brought to Shetland by traders. There is a romantic tale that the islanders copied the patterns from those worn by sailors of the Spanish Armada ship *El Gran Griffon*, which was wrecked on Fair Isle in 1588. Since this story seems to have originated in the middle of the nineteenth century, it seems more likely that the knitters were using a myth to boost the sale of their knitting to visitors.

The earliest examples of Fair Isle patterned knitting as we know it today, are a beautiful cap and purse dating from 1850, which can be seen in the National Museum of Antiquities of Scotland, in Edinburgh. These have large geometric patterns in coloured bands and are knitted in silk; it is possible they were made for the Victorian tourist trade to the islands. The patterns of the mid-nineteenth-century Fair Isle knitting often consist of large hexagonal shapes with different crosses and motifs within them; these are described as the traditional OXO patterns. In between are different small – or 'peerie' – patterns, each one having a different background colour.

The ingenuity of the individual knitters led to the invention of a large variety of patterns; and some knitters would pride themselves on never using the same one twice within a garment. All their designs are achieved by using just two colours of yarn in any one row, with the colour not in use being stranded along the back of the knitting. The resulting double thickness gives the fabric increased warmth.

The colours originally used were the natural shades of the sheep's wool, ranging from natural black through all the greys, browns, and fawns to the natural creamy white. Shetland sheep come in many different colours, unlike other breeds, and the colours have wonderful Shetland names – 'shaela' and 'sholmit' (shades of grey); 'eesit' and 'mooskit' (shades of fawn); 'mogit' and 'moorit' (shades of brown). The dyed colours were originally obtained from natural dyes, with madder providing red, indigo giving blue, and onion skin making a yellow-gold colour. The madder and indigo were imported, and were first used in Shetland around 1840. These were the colours used in all Fair Isle knitting until about 1920, when mill-dyed yarns from Scotland began to be more generally used.

Around 1900 the first all-over patterned Fair Isle sweaters appeared; until that time, the knitters were producing smaller items such as scarves, hats, gloves and stockings. These sweaters were seamless garments, knitted in the round, with the sleeves knitted down from the shoulder to the cuff, and were used as workwear by the local fishermen. However, a chance act resulted in the growth of a thriving industry.

In 1922, the knitters of Shetland sent a parcel of knitwear to Princess Mary, daughter of George V, on the occasion of her marriage. Apparently, the parcel included a Fair Isle patterned sweater, which came into the hands of her brother Edward, Prince of Wales (later Edward VIII and Duke of Windsor). The Prince wore the sweater at the Royal and Ancient Golf Club of St Andrews; and he then had his portrait painted by Sir Henry Lander wearing it. Fair Isle knitwear immediately became highly fashionable, and it remained popular until the Second World War.

Here you will find traditional patterns on a waistcoat, two slipovers, and two sweaters. One of the sweaters uses the natural Shetland colours and is knitted in the round; the other has a modern colourway using double knitting yarn, for those who want to produce a slightly heavier sweater. These old patterns make classic garments that will give years of pleasure and attract admiration wherever they are seen.

Cross and Flower Fair Isle Crew Neck

A traditional pattern takes on a new and bolder look when double knitting yarn is used in soft, woodland shades. Knitted in separate pieces and then seamed, this makes a warm sweater for either men or women. The design is based on the old OXO pattern and features striped ribs.

Cross and Square Fair Isle Slipover

This sleeveless slipover combines a bold, traditional pattern – a repeating cross motif – with more contemporary colours, which would suit either a man or a woman. It is knitted in the round in the Shetland way, which means that the pattern is always facing you as you work.

Diamond Fair Isle Waistcoat

A pretty waistcoat in a traditional pattern uses a modern colour scheme in lovely, soft moorland shades of Shetland wool, but another 4-ply yarn could be used. The pattern of 'shaded diamonds' or 'peaks' was very popular in the Fair Isle knitting of the 1940s.

Katie's Fair Isle Slipover

This old, intricate pattern uses the authentic Fair Isle colours of madder red and indigo blue and has rows of OXO, the Armada cross, and 'peerie' (little) patterns in between. It has become known as 'Katie's' pattern, after the knitter, and makes a slipover that is also suitable for men.

OXO Fair Isle Crew Neck

This beautiful old pattern was taken from a sweater owned by Margaret Stuart's grandmother, dating from about 1915. All the natural shades of the Shetland wool are used in the bold pattern. The striped ribbing, like the seamless construction, is another feature of real Fair Isle.

Cross and Flower Fair Isle Crew Neck

❋ MATERIALS

Yarn

Rowan pure wool DK (approx 125m/136 yards)
A 2 [2, 2, 3, 3] x 50g balls, shade 020 Parsley
B 2 [2, 2, 3, 3] x 50g balls, shade 021 Glade
C 2 [2, 2, 3, 3] x 50g balls, shade 015 Barley
D 2 [3, 3, 3, 3] x 50g balls, shade 016 Hessian
E 2 [2, 2, 2, 3] x 50g balls, shade 035 Quarry
F 3 [3, 3, 3, 4] x 50g balls, shade 007 Cypress

Needles

1 pair size 3.75mm
1 pair size 4.5mm

Notions

1 stitch holder

Special abbreviation

m1 Pick up loop lying between sts and k tbl

❋ MEASUREMENTS

To fit chest 86 [91, 97, 102, 107]cm
34 [36, 38, 40, 42]in
Actual chest size 96 [102, 106, 110, 116]cm
37¾ [40, 41¾, 43¼, 45½]in
Length to back neck 55 [59, 60, 62, 65]cm
21½ [23¼, 23½, 24¼, 25½]in
Sleeve seam 41 [42, 45, 48, 50]cm
16 [16½, 17¾, 19, 19¾]in

Tension

23 sts and 26 rows measure 10cm over
pattern on 4.5mm needles (or size needed
to obtain given tension)

Note

The motif in the pattern that falls in the
centre of the body and the sleeves may
vary from the photograph depending
on the size being knitted.

Row 1 (Right side) P2A, (k2B, p2A) to end.
Row 2 K2A, (p2B, k2A) to end.
Row 3 P2A, (k2C, p2A) to end.
Row 4 K2A, (p2C, k2A) to end.
Row 5 P2A, (k2D, p2A) to end.
Row 6 K2A, (p2D, k2A) to end.
Row 7 P2A, (k2E, p2A) to end.
Row 8 K2A, (p2E, k2A) to end.
Row 9 P2A, (k2F, p2A) to end.
Row 10 K2A, (p2F, k2A) to end.
Rows 11 and 12 As rows 7 and 8.
Rows 13 and 14 As rows 5 and 6.
Rows 15 and 16 As rows 3 and 4.
Rows 17 and 18 As rows 1 and 2.
Change to 4.5mm needles.
Next row Using yarn A, k5 [7, 9, 9, 7], *m1,
k16 [12, 12, 10, 9]; rep from * to last 5 [7, 9, 9,
7] sts, m1, k to end. *113 [119, 123, 129, 135] sts.*
P 1 row in A. Reading odd-numbered (k) rows
from right to left and even-numbered (p) rows
from left to right, cont in st st and patt from
chart until work measures 35 [37, 38, 40,
40]cm from beg ending with a wrong-side row.

Shape armholes

Cast off 12 [14, 14, 16, 16] sts at beg of next

---

2 rows. *89 [91, 95, 97, 103] sts.* Cont straight
in patt until armholes measure 20 [22, 22, 22,
25]cm, ending with a wrong-side row.

Shape shoulders

Next row Cast off 25 [25, 27, 27, 30] sts, patt
to last 25 [25, 27, 27, 30] sts. Cast off these
sts. Leave rem 39 [41, 41, 43, 43] sts on a
spare needle.

FRONT

Work as given for back until armholes
measure 10 [11, 11, 11, 13]cm, ending with
a wrong-side row.

Shape neck

Next row Patt 38 [38, 40, 41, 44] sts and
turn; leave rem sts on a spare needle.
Complete left side of neck first. Cast off 2 sts
at beg of next row and foll 3 alt rows then
1 st on every alt row until 25 [25, 27, 27, 30]
sts rem. Cont straight until front matches
back to shoulder, ending with a wrong-side
row. Cast off.
With right side facing, sl centre 13 [15, 15, 15,
15] sts on to stitch holder, rejoin appropriate
yarn to rem sts and patt to end. Patt 1 row.
Complete to match first side of neck.

SLEEVES

Using 3.75mm needles and yarn A, cast on 46
[46, 46, 50, 54] sts. Work 18 rows in rib as
given for back welt. Change to 4.5mm needles.
Next row Using A, k5 [7, 7, 7, 6], *m1, k3 [2, 2,
2, 3]; rep from * to last 2 [5, 5, 5, 3] sts, k to
end. *59 [63, 63, 69, 69] sts.*
P 1 row in A. Cont in st st and patt from chart
as given for 2nd [3rd, 3rd, 4th, 4th] sizes, inc
1 st at each end of 9th [1st, 9th, 9th, 3rd] row
and every foll 4th [4th, 4th, 5th, 5th] row until
there are 95 [103, 103, 103, 117] sts, working
extra sts into patt. Cont straight until sleeve
measures 41 [42, 45, 48, 50]cm. Mark each
end of last row. Work a further 5 [6, 6, 7, 7]cm
in patt, ending with a wrong-side row.
Cast off.

BACK

Carry yarn not in use loosely across wrong
side of work. Using 3.75mm needles and yarn
A, cast on 106 [110, 114, 118, 122] sts.

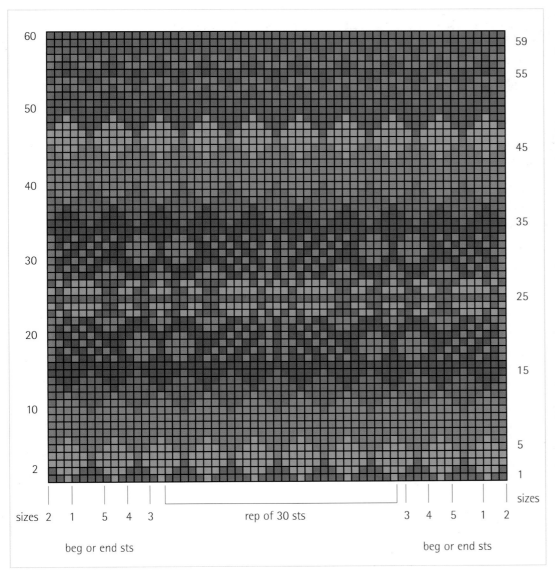

60

50

40

30

20

10

2

59

55

45

35

25

15

5

1

sizes 2 1 5 4 3   rep of 30 sts   3 4 5 1 2 sizes

beg or end sts   beg or end sts

NECKBAND

Join right shoulder seam. With right side facing, using 3.75mm needles and yarn A, pick up and k 23 [25, 27, 28, 30] sts down left side neck, k across 13 [15, 15, 15, 15] centre front sts, pick up and k 23 [25, 27, 28, 30] sts up right side neck, k across 39 [41, 41, 43, 43] centre back sts. *98 [106, 110, 114, 118] sts.* **Next row** (Wrong side) K2A, (p2D, k2A) to end. Now rep rows 13 and 18 as given for back welt. Using A, cast off in rib.

FINISHING

Block each piece as given on page 139. Join left shoulder and neckband seam. Sew in sleeves, sewing rows above markers to cast-off sts at armholes. Join side and sleeve seams.

Key

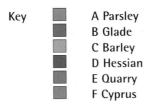

A Parsley
B Glade
C Barley
D Hessian
E Quarry
F Cyprus

Cross and Square Fair Isle Slipover

❋ MATERIALS

Yarn

Jamieson's Spindrift 2-ply jumper weight
(100% Shetland wool, approx 105m/115 yards)
A 4 [4, 4, 4] x 25g balls, shade 730 Dark Navy
C 2 [2, 2, 2] x 25g balls, shade 577 Chestnut
E 1 [1, 2, 2] x 25g balls, shade 763 Pacific
F 3 [3, 4, 4] x 25g balls, shade 179 Buttermilk
Jamieson and Smith's 2-ply jumper weight
(100% Shetland wool, approx 115m/125 yards)
B 1 [1, 2, 2] x 25g balls, shade FC14
(purple mix)
D 1 [1, 2, 2] x 25g balls, shade 4
(moorit brown)
G 1 [1, 2, 2] x 25g balls, shade 128 (red mix)

Needles

1 circular needle size 2.75mm, 60cm long
1 circular needle size 2.75mm, 40cm long
1 circular needle size 3mm, 80cm long

Special abbreviation

m1 Pick up loop lying between sts and k tbl

❋ MEASUREMENTS

To fit chest 86 [91, 97, 102]cm
34 [36, 38, 40]in
Actual chest size 97 [101, 109, 116]cm
38¼ [39¾, 43, 45¾]in
Length to back neck 55 [58, 61, 63]cm
21¾ [22¾, 24, 24¾]in

Tension

33 sts and 38 rows measure 10cm over
pattern on 3mm needles (or size needed
to obtain given tension)

BACK AND FRONT

This garment is knitted in one piece to the
armholes. Carry yarn not in use loosely across
wrong side of work. Using circular needle size
2.75mm, 60cm long and yarn A, cast on 276
[300, 320, 336] sts. Cont in rounds as follows:
Rounds 1–3 (K2B, p2A) to end.
Rounds 4–6 (K2C, p2A) to end.
Rounds 7–9 (K2D, p2A) to end.
Rounds 10–12 (K2E, p2A) to end.
Rounds 13–15 As rounds 7–9.
Rounds 16–18 As rounds 4–6.
Rounds 19–21 As rounds 1–3.
Change to circular needle size 3mm.
Next round Using A, *(k8, m1) 2 [2, 1, 1]
times, k7 [9, 8, 6], m1; rep from * to end.
312 [336, 360, 384] sts.
Reading rounds from right to left cont in st st
and patt from chart.
Cont in patt until work measures 35 [35, 38,
38]cm from beg, ending 1 [7, 14, 20] sts
before end of last round.

Divide for back and front

Next round *Cast off 21 [21, 23, 23], patt 135
[147, 157, 169] including st used in casting
off; rep from * once more.
Complete back first. Keeping continuity of
patt, work backwards and forwards in st st,
reading p rows from left to right from chart.
Next row Patt to end.
Next row K1, skpo, patt to last 3 sts, k2 tog, k1.
Rep last 2 rows until 109 [117, 127, 137] sts rem.
Next 3 rows Patt to end.
Next row K1, skpo, patt to last 3 sts, k2 tog, k1.
Rep last 4 rows 5 times more. *97 [105, 115,
125] sts.*
Cont straight until armhole measures 20 [23,
23, 25]cm, ending with a wrong-side row.

Shape shoulders

Next row Cast off 30 [32, 35, 40] sts, patt
to last 30 [32, 35, 40] sts, cast off these sts.
Leave rem 37 [41, 45, 45] sts on a spare
needle. With wrong side of front facing, rejoin
appropriate yarn to rem sts.
Next row Patt 67 [73, 78, 84] sts and turn;
leave rem sts on needle.
Complete right side of neck first.
Next row Skpo, patt to last 3 sts, k2 tog, k1.
Next row Patt to end.
Rep last 2 rows 4 [4, 4, 5] times more.
Next row Patt to last 3 sts, k2 tog, k1.
Next row Patt to end.
Next row Skpo, patt to last 3 sts, k2 tog, k1.
Next row Patt to end.
Rep last 4 rows 3 [4, 4, 4] times more.
Next 2 rows Patt to end.
Next row Skpo, patt to last 3 sts, k2 tog, k1.
Next row Patt to end.
Rep last 4 rows 5 times more. Keeping
armhole edge straight, cont to dec at neck
edge as before until 30 [32, 35, 40] sts rem.
Cont straight until front matches back to
shoulder, ending with a wrong-side row.
Cast off.
With wrong side of front facing, sl next st on
to safety pin, rejoin appropriate yarn to rem
sts and patt to end.
Next row K1, skpo, patt to last 2 sts, k2 tog.

Main colour combination

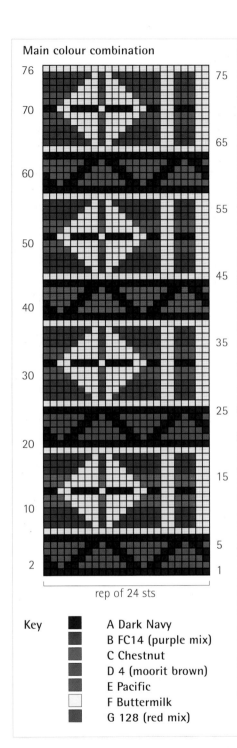

rep of 24 sts

Key

- A Dark Navy
- B FC14 (purple mix)
- C Chestnut
- D 4 (moorit brown)
- E Pacific
- F Buttermilk
- G 128 (red mix)

Next row Patt to end.
Rep last 2 rows 4 [4, 4, 5] times more.
Next row K1, skpo, patt to end.
Next row Patt to end.

Next row K1, skpo, patt to last 2 sts, k2 tog.
Next row Patt to end.
Rep last 4 rows 3 [4, 4, 4] times more.
Next 2 rows Patt to end.
Next row K1, skpo, patt to last 2 sts, k2 tog.
Next row Patt to end.
Complete as given for right side of neck.

NECKBAND

Join shoulder seams. With right side facing,
using circular needle size 2.75mm, 60cm long
and yarn A, pick up and k 76 [84, 84, 88] sts
down left side neck, k centre front st, pick up
and k 76 [84, 84, 88] sts up right side of neck,
k 18 [20, 22, 22] inc in next st, k 18 [20, 22, 22]
across centre back sts. *191 [211, 215, 223] sts.*
Round 1 (K2D, p2A) 18 [20, 20, 21] times,
k2D, using A, skpo, k1, k2 tog, (k2D, p2A) 28
[31, 32, 33] times.
Round 2 (K2D, p2A) 18 [20, 20, 21] times,
using D, k1, skpo, k1A, using D, k2 tog, k1D,
p2A, (k2D, p2A) 27 [30, 31, 32] times.
Round 3 (K2D, p2A) 18 [20, 20, 21] times,
using D, skpo, k1A, using D, k2 tog, p2A, (k2D,
p2A) 27 [30, 31, 32] times.
Round 4 (K2C, p2A) 17 [19, 19, 20] times,
k2C, using A, p1, ybk, skpo, k1, k2 tog, p1,
(k2C, p2A) 27 [30, 31, 32] times.
Round 5 (K2C, p2A) 17 [19, 19, 20] times,
k2C, using A, skpo, k1, k2 tog, (k2C, p2A) 27
[30, 31, 32] times.
Round 6 K2C, p2A) 17 [19, 19, 20] times,
using C, k1, skpo, k1A, using C, k2 tog, k1C,
p2A, (k2C, p2A) 26 [29, 30, 31] times.
Round 7 (K2B, p2A) 17 [19, 19, 20] times,
using B, skpo, k1A, using B, k2 tog, p2A, (k2B,
p2A) 26 [29, 30, 31] times.
Round 8 (K2B, p2A) 16 [18, 18, 19] times,
k2B, using A, p1, ybk, skpo, k1, k2 tog, p1,
(k2B, p2A) 26 [29, 30, 31] times.
Round 9 (K2B, p2A) 16 [18, 18, 19] times,
k2B, using A, skpo, k1, k2 tog, (k2B, p2A) 26
[29, 30, 31] times.
Using A, cast off in rib.

ARMBANDS

With right side facing, using circular needle
size 2.75mm, 40cm long, yarn A and beg at
centre of cast-off sts at armhole, pick up and
k 156 [168, 172, 184] sts evenly around
armhole edge. Work in rounds as follows:
Rounds 1–3 (K2D, p2A) to end.
Rounds 4–6 (K2C, p2A) to end.
Rounds 7–9 (K2B, p2A) to end.
Using A, cast off in rib.

FINISHING

Darn in any loose ends. Block as given on
page 139.

Diamond Fair Isle Waistcoat

❈ MATERIALS

Yarn

Jamieson and Smith's 2-ply jumper weight
(100% Shetland wool, approx 115m/125 yards)
A 4 [4, 5, 5] x 25g balls, shade FC14 (purple mix)
C 3 [3, 4, 4] x 25g balls, shade 141 (clan grey)
D 3 [3, 4, 4] x 25g balls, shade FC64 (fawn mix)
Jamieson's Spindrift 2-ply jumper weight
(100% Shetland wool, approx 105m/115 yards)
B 3 [3, 4, 4] x 25g balls, shade 577 Chestnut

Needles

1 pair size 2.75mm
1 pair size 3mm
1 circular needle size 2.75mm, 80cm long
1 circular needle size 2.75mm, 40cm long
1 circular needle size 3mm, 80cm long

Notions

5 buttons, 1.7cm in diameter
2 stitch holders

❈ MEASUREMENTS

To fit chest 86 [91, 97, 102]cm
34 [36, 38, 40]in
Actual chest size 97 [105, 112, 119]cm
38¼ [41¼, 44, 46¾]in
Length to back neck 56 [59, 62, 64]cm
22 [23¼, 24½, 25¼]in

Tension

33 sts and 38 rows measure 10cm over
pattern on 3mm needles (or size needed
to obtain given tension)

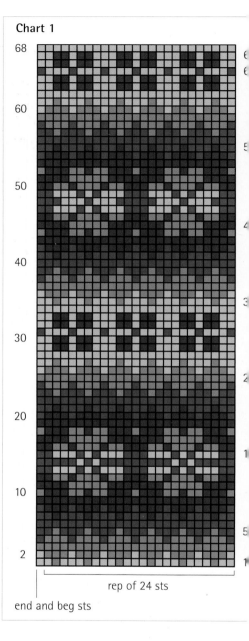

Chart 1

rep of 24 sts

end and beg sts

POCKET LININGS

Carry yarn not in use loosely across wrong
side of work. Using 3mm pair of needles and
yarn A, cast on 37 sts. Purl 1 row in D.

Reading odd-numbered (k) rows from right to
left and even-numbered (p) rows from left to
right and beg with a k row, cont in st st, work
36 rows from chart 2. Leave these sts on a spare
needle. Make another pocket lining to match.

MAIN PART

Using circular needle size 2.75mm, 80cm long
and A, cast on 310 [334, 358, 382] sts. Work
backwards and forwards as follows:
Row 1 (Right side) K2B, (p2A, k2B) to end.
Row 2 P2B, (k2A, p2B) to end.
Rows 3 and 4 As rows 1 and 2.
Row 5 K2C, (p2A, k2B) to end.
Row 6 P2C, (k2A, p2C) to end.
Rows 7 and 8 As rows 5 and 6.
Row 9 K2D, (p2A, k2D) to end.
Row 10 P2D, (k2A, p2D) to end.
Rows 11 and 12 As rows 9 and 10.
Rows 13–16 As rows 5–8.
Rows 17–20 As rows 1–4.
Change to circular needle size 3mm. K 1 row
in A, inc 3 sts evenly. 313 [337, 361, 385] sts.
P 1 row in D. Cont in st st and patt from chart
1, work 36 rows.
Place pocket

Next row Patt 25 sts, sl next 37 sts on to stitch
holder, patt across first pocket lining, patt to
last 62 sts, sl next 37 sts on to stitch holder,
patt across second pocket lining, patt to end.
Cont in patt until work measures 35 [35, 38,
38]cm from beg, ending with a wrong-side row.
Divide for armholes
Next row Patt 66 [72, 75, 81] sts, cast off
20 [20, 24, 24], patt 141 [153, 163, 175] sts
including st used in casting off, cast off

Chart 2

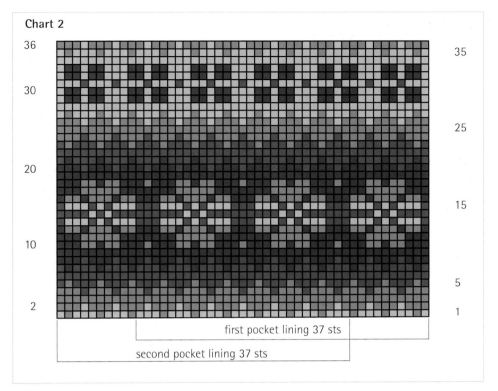

first pocket lining 37 sts

second pocket lining 37 sts

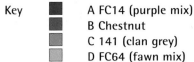
and yarn A, pick up and k 112 [112, 120, 120] sts up right front to front shaping, 73 [82, 82, 90] sts up shaped edge to shoulder, k 32 [35, 37, 39], k2 tog, k 31 [34, 36, 38] across back neck sts, pick up and k 73 [82, 82, 90] sts down shaped edge of left front and 112 [112, 120, 120] sts down left front.
434 [458, 478, 498] sts.
Work backwards and forwards as follows:
Row 1 (Wrong side) P2D, (k2A, p2D) to end.
Row 2 K2D, (p2A, k2D) to end.
Row 3 As row 1.
The last 2 rows form rib. Using C instead of D, cont in rib.
Row 4 Rib 4, *cast off 2, rib 24 [24, 26, 26]; rep from * 4 times more, rib to end.
Row 5 Rib to end, casting on 2 sts over those cast off in previous row. Rib 1 row. Using B instead of D, rib 3 rows. Using A, cast off in rib.

ARMBANDS

With right side facing, using circular needle size 2.75mm, 40cm long, yarn A and beg at centre of cast-off sts for armhole, pick up and k 156 [172, 172, 184] sts evenly around armhole edge. Work in rounds as follows:
Rounds 1–3 (K2D, p2A) to end.
Rounds 4–6 (K2C, p2A) to end.
Rounds 7–9 (K2B, p2A) to end.
Using A, cast off in rib.

POCKET EDGINGS

With right side facing, using 2.75mm needles, rejoin yarn A to the 37 sts on pocket top. K 1 row, inc 1 st at centre. *38 sts.*
Work 9 rows in rib as given for front band, omitting buttonholes. Using A, cast off in rib.

FINISHING

Darn in any lose ends. Block as given on page 139. Catch down pocket linings and sides of pocket edgings. Sew on buttons.

20 [20, 24, 24], patt to end.
Complete left front first. Keep continuity of patt.
Next row Patt to end.
Next row K1, skpo, patt to last 2 sts, k2 tog.
Rep last 2 rows 4 [5, 5, 5] times more.
Next row Patt to end.
Next row Patt to last 2 sts, k2 tog.
Next row Patt to end.
Next row K1, skpo, patt to last 2 sts, k2 tog.
Rep last 4 rows 3 times more. Keeping armhole edge straight, cont dec at neck edge as set on every foll alt row until 35 [39, 42, 47] sts rem, then on every foll 4th row until 29 [31, 34, 38] sts rem. Cont straight until armhole measures 20 [23, 23, 25]cm, ending at armhole edge.
Shape shoulder
Cast off 10 [10, 11, 13] sts at beg of next row and foll alt row. Work 1 row. Cast off rem 9 [11, 12, 12] sts.
With wrong side facing, rejoin appropriate yarn to 141 [153, 163, 175] sts for back.
Next row Patt to end.
Next row K1, skpo, patt to last 3 sts, k2 tog, k1.
Rep last 2 rows 4 [5, 5, 5] times more.

Next 3 rows Patt to end.
Next row K1, skpo, patt to last 3 sts, k2 tog, k1.
Rep last 4 rows 3 times more.
123 [133, 143, 155] sts.
Cont straight until armholes measure 20 [23, 23, 25]cm, ending with a wrong-side row.
Shape shoulders
Cast off 10 [10, 11, 13] sts at beg of next 4 rows and 9 [11, 12, 12] sts at beg of foll 2 rows. Leave rem 65 [71, 75, 79] sts on a spare needle.
With wrong side facing, rejoin appropriate yarn to rem 66 [72, 75, 81] sts for right front.
Next row Patt to end.
Next row Skpo, patt to last 3 sts, k2 tog, k1.
Rep last 2 rows 4 [5, 5, 5] times more.
Next row Patt to end.
Next row Skpo, patt to end.
Next row Patt to end.
Next row Skpo, patt to last 3 sts, k2 tog, k1.
Complete as given for left front.

BUTTON BAND

Join shoulder seams. With right side facing, using circular needle size 2.75mm, 80cm long

Katie's Fair Isle Slipover

❈ MATERIALS

Yarns

Jamieson's Spindrift 2-ply jumper weight
(100% Shetland wool, approx 105m/115 yards)
A 4 [4, 4, 4, 4] x 25g balls, shade 726
Prussian Blue
B 2 [2, 2, 2, 2] x 25g balls, shade 289
Fool's Gold
D 2 [2, 2, 2, 2] x 25g balls, shade 104
Natural White
E 3 [3, 3, 4, 4] x 25g balls, shade 577
Chestnut
Jamieson and Smith's 2-ply jumper weight
(100% Shetland wool, approx 115m/125 yards)
C 2 [2, 2, 2, 2] x 25g balls, shade 4
(moorit brown)
F 2 [2, 2, 2, 2] x 25g balls, shade 5
(Shetland black)

Needles

1 circular needle size 2.75mm, 40cm long
1 circular needle size 2.75mm, 60cm long
1 circular needle size 3mm, 80cm long

Special abbreviation

m1 Pick up loop lying between sts and k tbl

❈ MEASUREMENTS

To fit chest 86 [91, 97, 102, 107]cm
34 [36, 38, 40, 42]in
Actual chest size 92 [98, 104, 109, 114]cm
36¼ [38½, 41, 43, 45]in
Length to back neck 55 [58, 58, 61, 63]cm
21¾ [22¾, 22¾, 24, 24¾]in

Tension

33 sts and 38 rows measure 10cm over
pattern on 3mm needles (or size needed
to obtain given tension)

BACK AND FRONT

This garment is knitted in one piece to the
armholes. Carry yarn not in use loosely across
wrong side of work. Using circular needle size
2.75mm, 60cm long and yarn A, cast on 284
[300, 316, 332, 348] sts. Cont in rounds as
follows:

Rounds 1–4 (K2B, p2A) to end.
Rounds 5–8 (K2C, p2A) to end.
Rounds 9–12 (K2D, p2A) to end.
Rounds 13–16 (K2E, p2A) to end.
Rounds 17–24 As rounds 1–8.
Change to circular needle size 3mm.
Next round **Using A, k6 [9, 7, 5, 10], *m1, k13
[12, 12, 12, 11]; rep from * 9 [10, 11, 12, 13]
times more, m1, k6 [9, 7, 5, 10]**; rep from **
to ** once more. *306 [324, 342, 360, 378] sts.*
Cont in st st and patt as given on chart reading
rounds from right to left until work measures
35 [35, 35, 38, 38]cm from beg, finishing 10
[6, 11, 7, 12] sts before end of last round.

Divide for back and front

Next round *Cast off 20 [21, 22, 23, 24] sts,
patt 133 [141, 149, 157, 165] sts including st

used in casting off; rep from * once more.
Complete back first. Cont in st st and patt from
chart, reading p rows from left to right and
working backwards and forwards as follows:
Next row Patt to end.
Next row K1, skpo, patt to last 3 sts, k2 tog, k1.
Rep last 2 rows until 97 [105, 111, 119, 125]
sts rem. Cont straight until armholes measure
20 [23, 23, 23, 25]cm, ending with a wrong-
side row.

Shape shoulders

Next row Cast off 26 [30, 33, 37, 38] sts, patt
to last 26 [30, 33, 37, 38] sts, cast off these
sts. Leave rem 45 [45, 45, 45, 49] sts on a
spare needle. With wrong side facing, rejoin
appropriate yarn to rem sts.
Next row Patt 66 [70, 74, 78, 82] sts and turn
leaving rem sts on a spare needle.

Key

A Prussian Blue
B Fool's Gold
C 4 (moorit brown)
D Natural White
E Chestnut
F 5 (Shetland black)

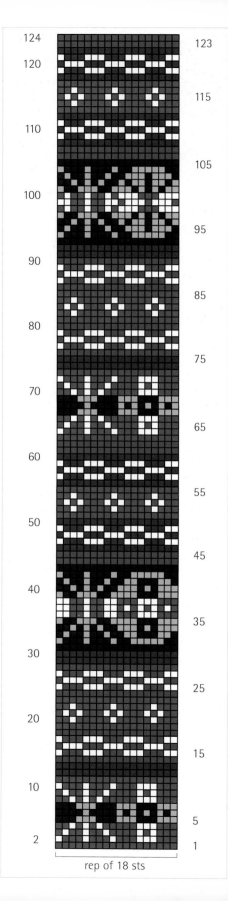

rep of 18 sts

NECKBAND

Join shoulder seams. With right side facing, using circular needle size 2.75mm, 60cm long and yarn A, pick up and k 76 [84, 84, 84, 88] sts down left side neck, k centre st on safety pin, pick up and k 76 [84, 84, 84, 88] sts up right side of neck, k across 45 [45, 45, 45, 49] centre back sts inc 1 st at centre.
199 [215, 215, 215, 227] sts.
Work in rounds as follows:
Round 1 (K2E, p2A) 18 [20, 20, 20, 21] times, k2E, using A, skpo, k1, k2 tog, k2E, (p2A, k2E) 30 [32, 32, 32, 34] times.
Round 2 (K2E, p2A) 18 [20, 20, 20, 21] times, k1E, using E, skpo, k1A, using E, k2 tog, k1, (p2A, k2E) 30 [32, 32, 32, 34] times.
Round 3 (K2D, p2A) 18 [20, 20, 20, 21] times, using D, skpo, k1A, using D, k2 tog, (p2A, k2D) 30 [32, 32, 32, 34] times.
Round 4 (K2D, p2A) 17 [19, 19, 19, 20] times, k2D, using A, p1, ybk, skpo, k1, k2 tog, p1, k2D, (p2A, k2D) 29 [31, 31, 31, 33] times.
Round 5 (K2C, p2A) 17 [19, 19, 19, 20] times, k2C, using A, skpo, k1, k2 tog, k2C, (p2A, k2C) 29 [31, 31, 31, 33] times.
Round 6 (K2C, p2A) 17 [19, 19, 19, 20] times, k1C, using C, skpo, k1A, using C, k2 tog, k1, (p2A, k2C) 29 [31, 31, 31, 33] times.
Round 7 (K2B, p2A) 17 [19, 19, 19, 20] times, using B, skpo, k1A, using B, k2 tog, (p2A, k2B) 29 [31, 31, 31, 33] times.
Round 8 (K2B, p2A) 16 [18, 18, 18, 19] times, k2B, using A, p1, ybk, skpo, k1, k2 tog, p1, k2B, (p2A, k2B) 28 [30, 30, 30, 32] times.
Using A, cast off in rib, dec as before.

ARMBANDS

With right side facing, using circular needle size 2.75mm, 40cm long, yarn A and beg at centre of cast-off sts at armhole, pick up and k 156 [168, 168, 168, 184] sts evenly around armhole edge. Work in rounds as follows:
Rounds 1 and 2 (K2E, p2A) to end.
Rounds 3 and 4 (K2D, p2A) to end.
Rounds 5 and 6 (K2C, p2A) to end.
Rounds 7 and 8 (K2B, p2A) to end.
Using yarn A, cast off in rib.

FINISHING

Darn in any loose ends. Block as given on page 139.

Complete right side of neck first.
Next row K2 tog, patt to last 3 sts, k2 tog, k1.
Next row Patt to end.
Rep last 2 rows 9 [5, 6, 6, 7] times more.
Next row Patt to last 3 sts, k2 tog, k1.
Next row Patt to end.
Next row K2 tog, patt to last 3 sts, k2 tog. k1.
Next row Patt to end.
Rep last 4 rows 3 [5, 5, 5, 5] times more.
Keeping armhole edge straight, cont dec at neck edge until 26 [30, 33, 37, 38] sts rem.
Cont straight until front matches back to shoulder, ending with a wrong-side row.
Cast off.
With wrong side of front facing, sl centre st on to a safety pin, rejoin appropriate yarn to rem sts and patt to end.
Next row K1, skpo, patt to last 2 sts, k2 tog.
Next row Patt to end.
Rep last 2 rows 9 [5, 6, 6, 7] times more.
Next row K1, skpo, patt to end.
Next row Patt to end.
Next row K1, skpo, patt to last 2 sts, k2 tog.
Next row Patt to end.
Complete as given for first side of neck.

OXO Fair Isle Crew Neck

✻ MATERIALS

Yarns
Jamieson and Smith's 2-ply jumper weight (100% Shetland wool, approx 115m/125 yards)
A 6 [7, 7, 7] x 25g balls, shade 5 (Shetland black)
B 2 [2, 3, 3] x 25g balls, shade 54 (dark grey)
C 2 [2, 2, 2] x 25g balls, shade 27 (mid grey)
D 7 [7, 7, 7] x 25g balls, shade 203 (light grey)
E 3 [3, 3, 3] x 25g balls, shade 202 (fawn)
F 4 [4, 4, 4] x 25g balls, shade 4 (moorit brown)

Needles
1 circular needle size 2.75mm, 60cm long
1 set of four double-pointed needles size 2.75mm
1 circular needle size 3mm, 80cm long
1 circular needle size 3mm, 40cm long

Notions
1 stitch holder

Special abbreviation
m1 Pick up loop lying between sts and k tbl

✻ MEASUREMENTS

To fit chest 86 [91, 97, 102]cm
34 [36, 38, 40]in
Actual chest size 96 [103, 109, 115]cm
37¾ [40½, 43, 45¼]in
Length to back neck 55 [58, 63, 65]cm
21¾ [22¾, 24¾, 25½]in
Sleeve seam 43 [45, 50, 50]cm
17 [17¾, 19¾, 19¾]in

Tension
33 sts and 38 rows measure 10cm over pattern on 3mm needles (or size needed to obtain given tension)

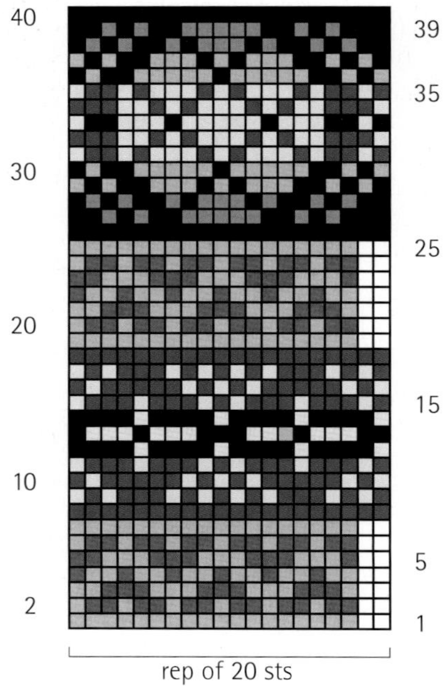

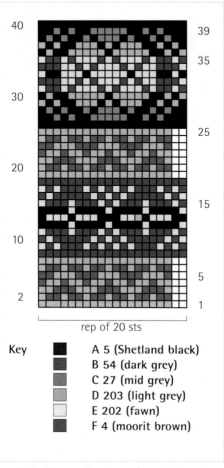

Key
- A 5 (Shetland black)
- B 54 (dark grey)
- C 27 (mid grey)
- D 203 (light grey)
- E 202 (fawn)
- F 4 (moorit brown)

Note The small patterns (rows 1–7 and 19–25) do not always fall in the same place in relation to the larger motifs.

BACK AND FRONT

This garment is knitted in one piece to the armholes. Carry yarn not in use loosely across wrong side of work.

Using circular needle size 2.75mm and yarn A, cast on 280 [300, 320, 340] sts. Cont in rounds as follows:

Rounds 1–3 (K2B, p2A) to end.
Rounds 4–6 (K2C, p2A) to end.
Rounds 7 and 8 (K2D, p2A) to end.
Rounds 9 and 10 (K2E, p2A) to end.
Rounds 11 and 12 As rounds 7 and 8.
Rounds 13–15 As rounds 4–6.
Rounds 16–18 As rounds 1–3.

Change to circular needle size 3mm, 80cm long.

Next round Using A, *k7 [7, 8, 8], m1, k7 [8, 8, 9], m1; rep from * to end. *320 [340, 360, 380] sts.*

Reading rounds from right to left and beg with round 19 [8, 1, 1] cont in st st and patt from chart until work measures 35 [38, 40, 40]cm from beg, ending with round 7 and 11 [7, 12, 8] sts before end of last round.

Divide for back and front

Next round *Cast off 23 [25, 25, 27], patt 137 [145, 155, 163] sts including st used in casting off; rep from * once more.

Complete back first. Keeping continuity of patt, work backwards and forwards in st st, reading p rows from left to right from chart.

Next row (Wrong side) Patt to end.
Next row K1, skpo, patt to last 3 sts, k2 tog, k1.

Rep last 2 rows until 107 [113, 123, 129] sts rem. Cont straight until armholes measure 20 [20, 23, 23]cm, ending with a wrong-side row.

Shape shoulders

Next row Cast off 29 [31, 34, 36] sts, patt to last 29 [31, 34, 36] sts, cast off these sts. Leave rem 49 [51, 55, 57] sts on a spare needle. With wrong side of front facing, rejoin appropriate yarn to rem sts.

Next row P1, p2 tog, patt to last 3 sts, p2 tog tbl, p1.
Next row K1, skpo, patt to last 3 sts, k2 tog, k1.

Rep last 2 rows 4 times more.

Next row Patt to end.
Next row K1, skpo, patt to last 3 sts, k2 tog, k1.

Rep last 2 rows until 107 [113, 123, 129] sts rem. Cont straight until armholes measure 13 [13, 15, 15]cm, ending with a wrong-side row.

Shape neck

Next row Patt 36 [38, 42, 44] and turn; leave rem sts on needle. Complete left side first.
Next row Patt to end.
Next row Patt to last 2 sts, k2 tog.

Rep last 2 rows until 29 [31, 34, 36] sts rem. Cont straight until front matches back to shoulder, ending with a wrong-side row. Cast off.

With right side of front facing, sl centre 35 [37, 39, 41] sts on to stitch holder, rejoin appropriate yarn to rem sts and patt to end.

Next row Patt to end.
Next row Skpo, patt to end.
Complete as given for left side neck.
Join shoulder seams.

SLEEVES

With right side facing, using circular needle size 3mm, 40cm long, yarn A and beg at centre of cast-off sts at armhole, pick up and k 140 [140, 160, 180] sts evenly around armhole edge. Cont in rounds of st st and patt from chart, working rounds in reverse order.
Rounds 1–7 As rounds 7–1.
Beg with round 40, cont in patt, work 15 [8, 15, 15] rounds.
Next round K1, k2 tog, patt to last 3 sts, skpo, k1. Patt 5 [6, 6, 5] rounds straight. Keeping continuity of patt, rep last 6 [7, 7, 6] rounds until 100 [100, 120, 130] sts rem, ending with dec round. Patt 5 [0, 11, 0] rounds straight.
Next round Using A, k8 [8, 0, 2], (k2 tog, k1) to last 8 [8, 0, 2] sts, k to end. *72 [72, 80, 88] sts.*
Change to set of four double-pointed needles

size 2.75mm. Work 18 rounds in rib as given for welt. Using A, cast off in rib.

NECKBAND

With right side facing, using set of four double-pointed needles size 2.75mm, pick up and k 22 [22, 25, 31] sts down left side neck, k across 35 [37, 39, 41] centre front sts, pick up and k 22 [22, 25, 31] sts up right side neck and k across 49 [51, 55, 57] centre back sts. *128 [132, 144, 160] sts.*
Round 1 (K2E, p2A) to end.
Rep this round 1 [1, 1, 2] times more.
Next round (K2D, p2A) to end.
Rep last round 1 [1, 2, 2] times more.
Next round (K2C, p2A) to end.
Rep last round 1 [2, 2, 2] times more.
Next 3 rounds (K2B, p2A) to end.
Using A, cast off in rib.

FINISHING

Darn in any loose ends. Block as given on page 139.

Aran

The Aran Islands lie off the west coast of Ireland in the mouth of Galway Bay, and are exposed to the Atlantic Ocean to the west – a position that has moulded their lifestyle and culture. There are three main islands: Inishmore (meaning the big island), Inishmaan (the middle island) and Inisheer (the west island). The cliffs can be steep and dangerous, the soil poor, and the sea rough; but in spite of this, the islanders for generations fished and farmed for a meagre livelihood. The landscape features tiny fields divided by dry stone walls, where they raise cattle and sheep. Because of their isolation, the islanders had to be as self-sufficient as possible. They spun their wool into yarn, and wove and knitted their own warm garments.

This lifestyle was portrayed in the film *Man of Aran*, which was released in 1934 and romanticized the reality of the lives of the islanders. Although ostensibly a documentary, the film was highly scripted, blurring fact with fiction. In particular, it portrayed scenes of hunting a shark in a way that had not been done for several generations.

The first supposed Aran sweater was discovered by a German called Heinz Kiewe in a shop in Dublin in the 1930s. In 1967 he published his book *The Sacred History of Knitting*, in which he developed a theory – now thought to be based largely on his imagination – that similar sweaters had been knitted in Aran for generations and created a myth that the patterns were ancient Celtic ones. Kiewe had never been to Aran, but his book was taken as gospel truth by many, and so the myth started to be believed as fact.

If we look at the oldest Aran sweaters, it seems more likely that these are related to the ganseys of the Scottish islands; perhaps a skilled knitter from Scotland brought her knowledge of stitch patterns to the Aran Island women. The knitting took on its distinctive local characteristics and became a cottage industry in the 1950s and 1960s, as it provided a source of income. By this time, the Aran sweater differed considerably from any original inspiration of Scottish ganseys. For one thing, the yarn was heavier, usually cream (natural white) and often oiled. The commercial consideration that this would knit up more quickly than fine wool probably had some influence here. Aran garments are now knitted in separate pieces, rather than in the round, but both methods were used by the earlier knitters, as is seen in the garments displayed in the National Museum in Dublin. Some garments in this museum feature fancy openwork patterns, which reinforces the idea that they are related to the openwork ganseys of the Western Isles of Scotland.

The Aran knitting that has become so popular today has a strong identity of its own, with features that distinguish it from other types of knitting. Perhaps the most important of these is the fact that nearly all the cables, diagonals making trellis or lattice patterns, and other patterns, are composed of plain knit stitches travelling across a purl stitch background; this has the result of raising the pattern into a texture of considerable depth. The use of bobbles enhances this embossed texture. The gansey, on the other hand, uses the opposite effect, having patterns raised on a plain stocking-stitch background.

Another difference between ganseys and Aran knits is that the stitch patterns in Aran nearly always run vertically, with no division between the body and yoke of the garment. Also, the sleeves are usually set in and the whole garment seamed. However, the two styles share many stitch patterns and motifs, such as Tree of Life and diamond, or lozenge, patterns. Cables, too, are common to both styles, but in Aran the cable is exploited to create many variations; for example, it can be divided into a lattice pattern or split to form a chevron.

Whether old or new, Aran knitting has now become part of the folk craft of Ireland and is today one of the most distinctive and recognizable knitting styles. The garments in this book show some of these stitches used in different weights of yarn and in different shapes, but all relate to what we know as the familiar Aran style of knitting.

Cable and Moss Aran Tunic

A contemporary design featuring traditional stitch patterns – medallion cable and moss stitch – this long, loose-fitting sweater is roomy enough to be worn over several layers of clothing and can replace a jacket on spring or autumn days in the country.

Chevron Aran Crew Neck

Classic Aran stitches – crossover chevron and moss stitch – are used on this roomy dropped-shoulder pullover. Shown here in the traditional natural white, it would look just as effective in the shade of your choice. The pattern is written in sizes to suit both women and men.

Tree of Life Aran Jacket

Two famous Aran patterns, the Tree of Life and chain cable, are worked into this woman's jacket. The Tree of Life is an ancient religious symbol, which is also said to represent family connections; the chain cable is related to the honeycomb pattern, a very old traditional pattern.

Wheat Cable Cotton Sweater

A delicate wheat-cable pattern used in two different combinations decorates this versatile cotton shirt-style sweater for relaxing in the country or wearing in the city. Elaborate, patterned welts at the hem and cuffs are interesting characteristics particular to Aran knitting.

Fountain Lace Short-Sleeve Sweater

The bold patterns of Aran are transformed in a fine 4-ply cotton yarn to make this delicate sweater, on which bands of fountain lace and plaited cable alternate. A neat collar and buttons at the back of the neck complete a classic, summery cotton top.

Classic Cotton Crew Neck

This traditional crew-neck sweater features a variety of stitch patterns, including a central honeycomb panel, Aran diamonds with moss stitch, and knotted chain cable. Either double-knitting-weight cotton, as here, or the same weight in wool can be used.

Cable and Moss Aran Tunic

❉ MATERIALS

Yarn

10 [11, 12] x 100g balls Rowan Pure
Wool Aran (approx 170m/186 yards),
shade 674 Cedar

Needles

1 pair size 4.5mm

1 pair size 5mm

1 cable needle

Special abbreviations

c4f Sl next 2 sts on to cable needle and
leave at front of work, k2 from left-hand
needle, k2 from cable needle

c4b Sl next 2 sts on to cable needle and
leave at back of work, k2 from left-hand
needle, k2 from cable needle

❉ MEASUREMENTS

To fit chest 91 [96, 102]cm

36 [38, 40]in

Actual chest size 106 [110, 116]cm

41¾ [43¼, 45¾]in

Length to back neck 66 [69, 72]cm

26 [27¼, 28¼]in

Sleeve seam 45cm, 18in

Tension

22 sts and 26 rows measure 10cm over
pattern on size 5mm needles (or size
needed to obtain given tension)

CABLE PANEL

Repeat of 13 sts.

Row 1 (Right side) P2, k9, p2.

Row 2 K2, p9, k2.

Rows 3 and 4 As rows 1 and 2.

Row 5 P2, c4f, k1, c4b, p2.

Row 6 As row 2.

Rows 7–12 Rep rows 1 and 2, 3 times.

Row 13 As row 5.

Row 14 As row 2.

Rows 15–20 Rep rows 1 and 2, 3 times.

Row 21 P2, c4b, k1, c4f, p2.

Row 22 As row 2.

Rows 23–26 Rep rows 1
and 2 twice.

These 26 rows form cable panel.

BACK

Using 4.5mm needles, cast
on 119 [123, 131] sts.

Row 1 (Right side) K1,
(p1, k1) to end.

Row 2 P1, (k1, p1)
to end.

Rep these two rows until rib
measures 5cm, ending with a
1st row. Purl 1 row. Change to
5mm needles. Commence patt.

Row 1 K1, (p1, k1) 8 [9, 11] times,
*work next 13 sts as 1st row of
cable panel, k1, (p2, k1) 5 times;
rep from * 3 times more, (p1, k1)
3 [4, 6] times.

Row 2 P1, (k1, p1) 8 [9, 11] times,
*work next 13 sts as 2nd row of
cable panel, p1, (k1, p1) 5 times; rep from *
3 times more, (k1, p1) 3 [4, 6] times.

Row 3 P1, (k1, p1) 8 [9, 11] times, *work next
13 sts as 3rd row of cable panel, p1, (k1, p1)
5 times; rep from * 3 times more, (p1, k1)
3 [4, 6] times.

Row 4 K1, (p1, k1) 8 [9, 11] times, *work
next 13 sts as 4th row of cable panel, k1, (p1,
k1) 5 times; rep from * 3 times more, (p1, k1)
3 [4, 6] times.

These 4 rows establish moss st patt.

Cont in patt as set, working appropriate rows
of cable panel until work measures 64 [67,
70]cm from beg, ending with a right-side row.

Shape neck

Next row Patt 42 [43, 46], cast off next 35
[37, 39] sts, patt to end.

Complete right side of back neck first. Dec
1 st at neck edge on every row until 37
[38, 41] sts rem. Patt 1 row. Cast off. With
right side facing, rejoin yarn to rem sts, k2
tog, patt to end. Complete to match first
side of neck.

POCKET LININGS

Using 5mm needles, cast on 31 sts. Beg k row,
work 15cm in st st, ending with a p row. Leave
these sts on a spare needle.

Make another pocket lining to match.

FRONT

Work as given for back until work measures
20cm, ending with a wrong-side row.

Place pockets

Next row Patt 10 [12, 16], sl next 31 sts on
to a stitch holder, patt across 31 sts of first
pocket lining, patt 37, sl next 31 sts on to
a stitch holder, patt across 31 sts of second
pocket lining, patt to end.

Cont in patt until front measures 59 [62,
65]cm from beg, ending with a right-side row.

Shape neck

Next row Patt 46 [47, 50], cast off next 27
[29, 31] sts, patt to end.

Complete left side of neck first. Dec 1 st at

neck edge on every row until 37 [38, 41] sts rem. Cont straight until front matches back to shoulder, ending with a wrong-side row. Cast off. With right side facing, rejoin yarn to rem sts, k2 tog, patt to end. Complete to match first side of neck.

SLEEVES

Using 4.5mm needles, cast on 59 sts. Work 5cm in rib as given for back welt, ending with a first row.
Next row P2, (inc in next st, p4) to last 2 sts, inc in next st, p1. *71 sts.*
Change to 5mm needles. Commence patt.
Row 1 K1, (p1, k1) twice, *work next 13 sts as 1st row of cable panel, k1, (p1, k1) 5 times; rep from * once more, work next 13 sts as 1st row of cable panel, k1, (p1, k1) twice.
Row 2 P1, (k1, p1) twice, *work next 13 sts as 2nd row of cable panel, p1, (p1, k1) 5 times; rep from * once more, work next 13 sts as 2nd row of cable panel, p1, (k1, p1) twice.
Row 3 P1, (k1, p1) twice, *work next 13 sts

as 3rd row of cable panel, p1, (k1, p1) 5 times; rep from * once more, work next 13 sts as 3rd row of cable panel, p1, (k1, p1) twice.
Row 4 K1, (p1, k1) twice, *work next 13 sts as 4th row of cable panel, k1, (p1, k1) 5 times; rep from * once more, work next 13 sts as 4th row of cable panel, k1, (p1, k1) twice.
These 4 rows establish moss st patt.
Cont in patt as set, working appropriate rows of cable panel. Inc 1 st at each end of next row and 8 foll 3rd rows, then on every foll 4th row until there are 117 sts, working extra sts into moss st patt. Cont straight until sleeve measures 44cm from beg, ending with a wrong-side row. Beg p row, work 2 rows st st. Cast off.

NECKBAND

With right side facing, join right shoulder seam. With right side facing and using 4.5mm needles, pick up and k 20 sts down left side of front neck, 25 [27, 29] sts from centre front, 20 sts up right side of front neck, 6 sts down

right side of back neck, 32 [34, 36] sts from centre back and 63 sts up left side of back neck. *109 [113, 117] sts.*
Beg 2nd row, work 12 rows in rib as for back welt. Cast off in rib.

POCKET EDGINGS

With right side facing and using 4.5mm needles, rejoin yarn to the 31 sts left on holder. Beg with a 1st row, work 6 rows in rib as given for back welt.
Cast off in rib.

FINISHING

Block each piece as given on page 139. With right side facing, join left shoulder seam. Fold neckband in half to wrong side and slipstitch. Catch down pocket linings and sides of pocket edgings. Mark position of armholes 26cm down from shoulders on back and front. Sew in sleeves between markers. Join side and sleeve seams.

Chevron Aran Crew Neck

❊ MATERIALS

Yarn

9 [9, 10] x 100g balls Rowan Pure Wool Aran
(approx 170m/186 yards), shade 670 Ivory

Needles

1 pair size 4mm

1 pair size 5mm

1 cable needle

Special abbreviations

cr5 Sl next 3 sts on to cable needle and
leave at back of work, k2 from left-hand
needle then p1, k2 from cable needle

cr3r Sl next st on to cable needle and leave
at back of work, k2 from left-hand needle,
p1 from cable needle

cr3l Sl next 2 sts on to cable needle and
leave at front of work, p1 from left-hand
needle, k2 from cable needle

❊ MEASUREMENTS

To fit chest 91 [97, 102]cm

36 [38, 40]in

Actual chest size 112 [116, 124]cm

44 [45¾, 48¾]in

Length to shoulder 66 [69, 72]cm

26 [27¼, 28¼]in

Sleeve seam 44cm, 17¼in

Tension

21 sts and 23 rows measure 10cm over pattern on 5mm needles (or size needed
to obtain given tension)

PATTERN PANEL

Worked over 19 sts.

Row 1 (Right side) K1 tbl, p6, k2, p1, k2, p6, k1 tbl.

Row 2 P1, k6, p2, k1, p2, k6, p1.

Row 3 K1 tbl, p6, cr5, p6, k1 tbl.

Row 4 As row 2.

Row 5 K1 tbl, p5, cr3r, k1, cr3l, p5, k1 tbl.

Row 6 P1, k5, p2, k1, p1, k1, p2, k5, p1.

Row 7 K1 tbl, p4, cr3r, k1, p1, k1, cr3l, p4, k1 tbl.

Row 8 P1, k4, p2, (k1, p1) twice, k1, p2, k4, p1.

Row 9 K1 tbl, p3, cr3r, (k1, p1) twice, k1, cr3l,
p3, k1 tbl.

Row 10 P1, k3, p2, (p1, k1) 3 times, k1, p2, k3, p1.

Row 11 K1 tbl, p2, cr3r, (k1, p1) 3 times, k1,
cr3l, p2, k1 tbl.

Row 12 P1, k2, p2, (k1, p1) 4 times, k1, p2, k2, p1.

Row 13 K1 tbl, p1, cr3r, (k1, p1) 4 times, k1,
cr3l, p1, k1 tbl.

Row 14 P1, k1, p2, (k1, p1) 5 times, k1, p2, k1, p1.

Row 15 K1 tbl, p1, k2, p3, k2, p1, k2, p3, k2,
p1, k1 tbl.

Rows 2–15 form panel pattern.

BACK

Using 4mm needles, cast on 110 [114, 118] sts.

Row 1 (Right side) K2, (p2, k2) to end.

Row 2 P2, (k2, p2) to end.

Rep these 2 rows until rib measures 10cm,
ending with row 1.

Next row Rib 5 [7, 3], *inc in next st, rib 9 [9,
7]; rep from * to last 5 [7, 3] sts, inc in next st,
rib to end. *121 [125, 133] sts.*

Change to 5mm needles. Commence patt.

Row 1 K1, (p1, k1) 5 [6, 8] times, *p2, work
row 1 of panel patt, p2, k1, (p1, k1) 7 times;
rep from * once more, p2, work row 1 of panel
patt, p2, (k1, p1) 5 [6, 8] times, k1.

Row 2 P1, (k1, p1) 5 [6, 8] times, *k2, work
row 2 of panel patt, k2, p1, (k1, p1) 7 times;
rep from * once more, k2, work row 2 of panel
patt, k2, (p1, k1) 5 [6, 8] times, p1.

Row 3 P1, (k1, p1) 5 [6, 8] times, *p2, work
3rd row of panel patt, p3, (k1, p1) 7 times; rep
from * once more, p2, work row 3 of panel
patt, p2, (p1, k1) 5 [6, 8] times, p1.

Row 4 K1, (p1, k1) 5 [6, 8] times, *k2, work
row 4 of panel patt, k3, (p1, k1) 7 times; rep
from * once more, k2, work row 4 of panel
patt, k2, (k1, p1) 5 [6, 8] times, k1.

These 4 rows establish moss st patt. Cont in
patt as set, working appropriate rows of panel
patt until work measures 63 [66, 69]cm from

beg, ending with a wrong-side row.

Shape neck

Next row Patt 49 [51, 53] sts and turn; leave
rem sts on a spare needle. Complete right side
of neck first. Dec 1 st at neck edge on next 5
rows. *44 [46, 48] sts.*

Patt 2 rows. Cast off.

With right side facing, sl centre 23 [23, 27] sts
on to a holder, rejoin yarn to rem sts and patt
to end. Complete to match first side of neck.

FRONT

Work as given for back until work measures
58 [61, 64]cm from beg, ending with a wrong-
side row.

Shape neck

Next row Patt 49 [51, 53] sts and turn; leave
rem sts on a spare needle. Complete left side
of neck first.

Dec 1 st at neck edge on next 5 rows. *44 [46,
48] sts.* Cont straight until front matches back
to shoulder, ending with a wrong-side row.

Cast off.
With right side facing, sl centre 23 [23, 27] sts on to holder, rejoin yarn to rem sts and patt to end. Complete to match first side of neck.

SLEEVES

Using 4mm needles, cast on 54 sts. Work 10cm in rib as given for back welt, ending with a 1st row.
Next row Rib 3 (inc in next st, rib 2) to end. *71 sts.*
Change to 5mm needles. Commence patt.
Row 1 K1, (p1, k1) twice, p2, work row 1 of panel patt, p2, k1, (p1, k1) 7 times, p2, work row 1 of panel patt, p2, (k1, p1) twice, k1.
Row 2 P1, (k1, p1) twice, k2, work row 2 of panel patt, k2, p1, (k1, p1) 7 times, k2, work row 2 of panel patt, k2, (p1, k1) twice, p1.

Row 3 P1, (k1, p1) twice, p2, work row 3 of panel patt, p3, (k1, p1) 7 times, p2, work row 3 of panel patt, p2, (p1, k1) twice, p1.
Row 4 K1, (p1, k1) twice, k2, work row 4 of panel patt, k3, (p1, k1) 7 times, k2, work row 4 of panel patt, k2, (k1, p1) twice, k1.
These 4 rows establish moss st patt. Cont in patt as set, working appropriate rows of panel patt, inc 1 st at each end of next row and every foll 4th row until there are 109 sts, working extra sts into moss st patt. Patt 1 row. Work should measure 43cm. Purl 1 row. Knit 1 row. Cast off.

NECKBAND

Join right shoulder seam. With right side facing and using 4mm needles, pick up and k 20 sts down left side of front neck, k 23 [23, 27] centre front sts, pick up and k 20 sts up right side of front neck, 8 sts down right side of back neck, k 23 [23, 27] centre back sts, pick up and k 8 sts up left side of back neck. *102 [102, 110] sts.*
Beg 2nd row, work 15 rows in rib as given for back welt. Cast off in rib.

FINISHING

Block each piece as given on page 139. Join left shoulder and neckband seam. Fold neckband in half to wrong side and slipstitch in place. Mark positions of armholes 25cm down from shoulders on back and front. Sew in sleeves. Join side and sleeve seams.

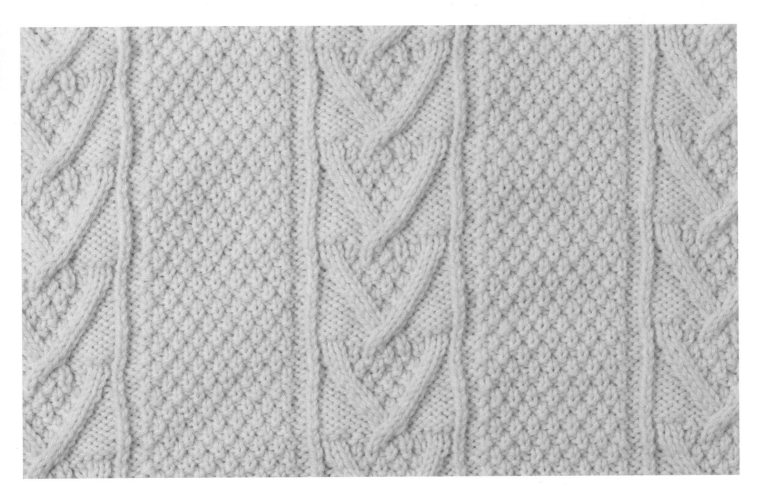

Tree of Life Aran Jacket

❊ MATERIALS

Yarn

10 [10, 10, 11] x 100g balls Rowan Pure Wool Aran (approx 170m/186 yards), shade 675 Sage

Needles

1 pair size 3.75mm

1 pair size 4.5mm

1 cable needle

Notions

3 buttons, 2.5cm in diameter

3 stitch holders

Special abbreviations

c4f Sl next 2 sts on to cable needle and leave at front of work, k2 from left-hand needle, k2 from cable needle

c4b Sl next 2 sts on to cable needle and leave at back of work, k2 from left-hand needle, k2 from cable needle

cr2r Sl next st on to cable needle and leave at back of work, k1, p1 from cable needle

cr2l Sl next st on to cable needle and leave at front of work, p1, k1 from cable needle

tw2 K into front of 2nd st then k first 2, sl both sts off needle tog

❊ MEASUREMENTS

To fit chest 81–86 [91–96, 102–107, 112–116]cm

32–34 [36–38, 40–42, 44–46]in

Actual chest size 105 [114, 126, 138]cm

41¼ [45, 49½, 54¼]in

Length to back neck 65 [66, 67, 68]cm

25½ [26, 26¼, 26¾]in

Sleeve seam 42 [43, 43, 44]cm

16½ [17, 17, 17¼]in

Tension

20 sts and 26 rows measure 10cm over pattern on 4.5mm needles (or size needed to obtain given tension)

CABLE PANEL

Repeat of 8 sts.

Row 1 (Wrong side) P8.

Row 2 C4b, c4f.

Row 3 P8.

Row 4 K8.

Row 5 P8.

Row 6 C4f, c4b.

Rows 7 and 8 As rows 3 and 4.

These 8 rows form cable panel.

TREE OF LIFE PANEL

Repeat of 12 sts.

Row 1 (Wrong side) K4, p4, k4.

Row 2 P3, cr2r, tw2, cr2l, p3.

Row 3 K3, (p1, k1, p1) twice, k3.

Row 4 P2, cr2r, p1, tw2, p1, cr2l, p2.

Row 5 K2, (p1, k2, p1) twice, k2.

Row 6 P1, cr2r, p2, tw2, p2, cr2l, p1.

Row 7 K1, (p1, k3, p1) twice, k1.

Row 8 Cr2r, p3, tw2, p3, cr2l.

These 8 rows form Tree of Life panel.

POCKET LININGS

Using 4.5mm needles, cast on 24 sts. Work 12cm in st st, ending with a p row.

Next row (K1, inc in next st, k1) to end. *32 sts.*

Leave these sts on a spare needle. Make another pocket lining to match.

BREAST POCKET LINING

Using 4.5mm needles, cast on 16 sts. Work 8cm in st st, ending with a p row.

Next row (K2, inc in next st, k1) to end. *20 sts.*

Leave these sts on a spare needle.

LEFT FRONT

Using 3.75mm needles, cast on 41 [45, 50, 56] sts.

Row 1 (Right side) K1 [1, 0, 0] tbl, (p1, k1 tbl) to end.

Row 2 (P1, k1 tbl) to last 1 [1, 0, 0] sts, p1 [1, 0, 0].

Rep these two rows once.

1st and 2nd sizes

***Next row** (Rib 1, inc in next st) 3 times, *rib 4 [5], inc in next st, rib 2, inc in next st, rib 4 [5], inc in next st, (rib 1, inc in next st) twice; rep from * once more, rib 1. *54 [58] sts.*

Change to 4.5mm needles. Commence patt.

Row 1 (Wrong side) K1, *work row 1 of cable panel, k1 [2], work row 1 of Tree of Life panel, k1 [2]; rep from * once more, work row 1 of cable panel, k1.

Row 2 P1, work row 2 of cable panel, *p1 [2], work row 2 of Tree of Life panel, p1 [2], work

Aran **101**

row 2 of cable panel; rep from * once more, p1***.

3rd and 4th sizes
Next row (Rib 1, inc in next st) 3 times, *rib [4, 5], inc in next st, rib 2, inc in next st, rib [4, 5], inc in next st, (rib 1, inc in next st) twice; rep from * once more, rib [3, 4], inc in next st, rib 2, inc in next st, rib [3, 4]. *[65, 71] sts.*
Change to 4.5mm needles. Commence patt.
Row 1 (Wrong side) K [0, 1], work row 1 of Tree of Life panel, k [0, 1], *work row 1 of cable panel, k [1, 2], work row 1 of Tree of Life panel, k [1, 2]; rep from * once more, work row 1 of cable panel, k1.
Row 2 P1, work row 2 of cable panel, *p [1, 2], work row 2 of Tree of Life panel, p [1, 2], work row 2 of cable panel; rep from * once more, p [0, 1], work row 2 of Tree of Life panel, p [0, 1].

All sizes
These 2 rows establish patt. Cont in patt as set, working appropriate rows of panels, patt 11 rows.
Dec row Patt 9, p2 tog, patt to end. Patt 11 rows straight.
Dec row Patt 20 [22, 20, 22], p2 tog, patt to end. Patt 5 rows straight.

Place pocket
Next row Patt 11 [14, 19, 23] sts, sl next 32 sts on to a stitch holder, patt across 32 sts of pocket lining, patt to end.
Patt 5 rows straight.
Dec row Patt 29 [31, 29, 31], p2 tog, patt to end. Patt 11 rows straight.
Dec row Patt 40 [44, 40, 44], p2 tog, patt to end. *50 [54, 61, 67] sts.*
Patt 5 rows straight.

Shape front
Dec 1 st at end of next row of 6 foll 8th rows. Patt 1 row. Work should measure 42cm from beg.

Shape armholes
Cast off 9 sts at beg of next row. Patt 1 row.

Place breast pocket
Next row Work 2 tog, patt 5 [7, 11, 14] , sl next 20 sts on to a stitch holder, patt across breast pocket lining, patt to end. Cont dec 1 st at front edge on foll 4th row and 2 [2, 4, 5] foll 8th rows and at the same time dec 1 st at armhole edge on foll 7 [11, 10, 12] alt rows. *23 [23, 29, 32] sts.*
Cont straight until armhole measures 21 [22,

23, 24]cm, ending at armhole edge.

Shape shoulder
Cast off 8 [8, 10, 11] sts at beg of next row and foll alt row. Patt 1 row. Cast off rem 7 [7, 9, 10] sts.

RIGHT FRONT

Using 3.75mm needles, cast on 41 [45, 50, 56] sts. Work 4 rows in rib as given for left front welt.

1st and 2nd sizes
Work as given for left front from *** to ***.

3rd and 4th sizes
Next row Rib [3, 4], inc in next st, rib 2, inc in next st, rib [3, 4], inc in next st, (rib 1, inc in next st) twice, *rib [4, 5], inc in next st, rib 2, inc in next st, rib [4, 5], inc in next st, (rib 1, inc in next st) twice; rep from * once more, rib 1. *[65, 71] sts.*
Change to 4.5mm needles. Commence patt.
Row 1 (Wrong side) K1, work row 1 of cable panel, *k [1, 2], work row 1 of Tree of Life panel, k [1, 2], work row 1 of cable panel; rep from * once more, k [0, 1], work row 1 of Tree of Life panel, k [0, 1].
Row 2 P [0, 1], work row 2 of Tree of Life panel, p [0, 1], work row 2 of cable panel, *p [1, 2], work row 2 of Tree of Life panel, p [1, 2], work row 2 of cable panel; rep from * once more, p1.

All sizes
These 2 rows establish patt. Cont in patt as set, working appropriate rows of panels, patt 11 rows.
Dec row Patt to last 11 sts, p2 tog tbl, patt to end. Patt 11 rows straight.
Dec row Patt to last 22 [24, 22, 24] sts, p2 tog tbl, patt to end.
Patt 5 rows straight.

Place pocket
Next row Patt 9 [10, 12, 14], sl next 32 sts on to a stitch holder, patt across 32 sts of pocket lining, patt to end.
Patt 5 rows straight.
Dec row Patt to last 31 [33, 31, 33] sts, p2 tog tbl, patt to end.
Patt 11 rows straight.
Dec row Patt to last 42 [46, 42, 46] sts, p2 tog tbl, patt to end. *50 [54, 61, 67] sts.*
Patt 5 rows straight.

Shape front
Dec 1 st at beg of next row and 6 foll 8th rows. Patt 2 rows.
Shape armhole Cast off 9 sts at beg of next row.
Next row Patt to last 2 sts, work 2tog. Complete as given for left front.

BACK

Using 3.75mm needles, cast on 90 [100, 105, 117] sts. Work 4 rows in rib as given for 3rd [3rd, 1st, 1st] sizes on left front welt.
Next row (Rib 1, inc in next st) 3 times, *rib 4 [5, 4, 5], inc in next st, rib 2, inc in next st, rib 4 [5, 4, 5], inc in next st, (rib 1, inc in next st) twice*; rep from * to * once more, **rib 3 [4, 3, 4], inc in next st, rib 2, inc in next st, rib 3 [4, 3, 4], inc in next st, (rib 1, inc in next st) twice **; rep from ** to ** 0 [0, 1, 1,] time more, now rep from * to * twice, rib 1. 118 [128, 138, 150] sts.
Change to 4.5mm needles. Commence patt.
Row 1 (Wrong side) K1, work row 1 of cable panel, *k1 [2, 1, 2], work row 1 of Tree of Life panel, k1 [2, 1, 2], work row 1 of cable panel*; rep from * to * once more, **k0 [1, 0, 1], work row 1 of Tree of Life panel, k0 [1, 0, 1], work row 1 of cable panel**; rep from ** to ** 0 [0, 1, 1,] time more, rep from * to * twice, k1.
Row 2 P1, work row 2 of cable panel, *p1 [2, 1, 2], work row 2 of Tree of Life panel, p1 [2, 1, 2], work row 2 of cable panel*; rep from * to * once more, **p0 [1, 0, 1], work row 2 of Tree of Life panel, p0 [1, 0, 1], work row 2 of cable panel**; rep from ** to ** 0 [0, 1, 1] time more, now rep from * to * twice, p1. These 2 rows establish patt. Cont in patt as set, working appropriate rows of panels, patt 11 rows.
Dec row Patt 9, p2 tog, patt to last 11 sts, p2 tog tbl, patt to end.
Patt 11 rows straight.
Dec row Patt 20 [22, 20, 22], p2 tog, patt to last 22 [24, 22, 24] sts, p2 tog tbl, patt to end.
Patt 11 rows straight.
Dec row Patt 29 [31, 29, 31], p2 tog, patt to last 31 [33, 31, 33] sts, p2 tog tbl, patt to end.
Patt 11 rows straight.
Dec row Patt 40 [44, 40, 44], p2 tog, patt to last 42 [46, 42, 46] sts, p2 tog tbl, patt to end. *110 [120, 130, 142] sts.*
Cont straight in patt until back matches front to

armhole shaping, ending with a wrong-side row.

Shape armholes
Cast off 9 sts at beg of next 2 rows. Dec 1 st at each end of next row and every foll alt row until 74 [78, 90, 98] sts rem. Cont straight until back matches front to shoulder ending with a wrong-side row.

Shape shoulders
Cast off 8 [8, 10, 11] sts at beg of next 4 rows and 7 [7, 9, 10] sts at beg of foll 2 rows. Cast off rem 28 [32, 32, 34] sts.

SLEEVES

Using 3.75mm needles, cast on 49 sts. Work 4 rows in rib as given for first size on left front welt.
Next row Rib 7, *(inc in next st, rib 1) 3 times, (rib 2, inc in next st) twice, rib 3; rep from * once more, (inc in next st, rib 1) 3 times, rib 6. *62 sts.*
Change to 4.5mm needles. Commence patt.
Row 1 (Wrong side) P3, k4, (work row 1 of cable panel then row 1 of Tree of Life panel) twice, work row 1 of cable panel, k4, p3.
Row 2 Tw2, cr2l, p3, (work row 2 of cable panel then row 2 of Tree of Life panel) twice, work row 2 of cable panel, p3, cr3r, tw2.
These 2 rows establish patt. Cont in patt as set, working appropriate rows of panels and inc 1 st at each end of 3rd row and every foll 7th [6th, 5th, 5th] row until there are 86 [90, 94, 96] sts, working extra sts into patt. Cont straight until sleeve measures 42 [43, 43, 44]cm from beg, ending with a wrong-side row.
Shape top Cast off 9 sts at beg of next 2 rows. Dec 1 st at each end of next row and every foll alt row until 50 sts rem then on every row until 16 sts rem. Cast off.

BUTTON BANDS AND COLLAR

Button band and collar
Join shoulder seams. Using 3.75mm needles, cast on 11 sts. Work in rib as given for first size on left front until band when slightly stretched fits along left front to front shaping, ending with a wrong-side row.

Shape collar
Cont in rib, inc 1 st at beg of next row and every foll alt row until there are 28 sts then on every foll 4th row until there are 34 [34, 36, 36] sts. Cont straight until collar fits along shaped edge of front to centre back neck. Cast off in rib. Sew in position.

Buttonhole band and collar
Mark button band with pins to indicate buttons, first one to come 2cm up from cast on edge and last one 3cm below beg of collar shaping, rem one spaced equally between. Work as given for button band, reversing collar shaping and working buttonholes at pin positions as follows:
Buttonhole row Rib 5, cast off 2, rib to end.
Next row Rib to end, casting on 2 sts over those cast off in previous row.
Sew in position then join back seam of collar.

POCKET EDGINGS

With right side facing and using 3.75mm needles, rejoin yarn to the 32 sts left on stitch holder.
Next row K1 tbl, p1, (k1 tbl, p1, k1 tbl, p2 tog) 5 times, (k1 tbl, p1) twice, k1 tbl. *27 sts.*
Beg 2nd row, work 7 rows in rib as given for first size on left front welt. Cast off in rib.

Breast pocket edging
With right side facing and using 3.75mm needles, rejoin yarn to the 20 sts left on stitch holder.
Next row K1 tbl, p1, (k1 tbl, p1, k1 tbl, p2 tog) 3 times, k1 tbl, p1, k1 tbl. *17 sts.*
Beg 2nd row, work 3 rows in rib as given for first size on left front welt. Cast off in rib.

FINISHING

Block each piece as given on page 139. Catch down pocket linings and sides of pocket edgings. Join side and sleeve seams. Sew in sleeves. Sew on buttons.

Wheat Cable Cotton Sweater

MATERIALS

Yarn
5 [5, 6, 6] x 100g balls Patons 100% mercerised cotton 4-ply (330m/361 yards),
shade 1716 Limestone

Needles
1 pair size 2.75mm
1 pair size 3.25mm
1 cable needle

Notions
4 buttons 1cm in diameter

Special abbreviations
c4f Sl next 2 sts on to cable needle and
leave at front of work, k2 from left-hand
needle, k2 from cable needle
c4b Sl next 2 sts on to cable needle and
leave at back of work, k2 from left-hand
needle, k2 from cable needle
cr3r Sl next st on to cable needle and leave
at back of work, k2 from left-hand needle,
p1 from cable needle
cr3l Sl next 2 sts on to cable needle and
leave at front of work, p1 from left-hand
needle, k2 from cable needle

MEASUREMENTS
To fit chest 81 [86, 91, 97]cm
32 [34, 36, 38]in
1 Actual chest size 92 [96, 102, 106]cm
36¼ [37¾, 40¼, 41¾]in
Length to back neck 61 [61, 62, 62]cm
24 [24, 24½, 24½]in
Sleeve seam 44 [45, 46, 47]cm
17¼ [17¾, 18, 18½]in

Tension
32 sts and 36 rows measure 10cm over
pattern on 3.25mm needles (or size needed
to obtain given tension)

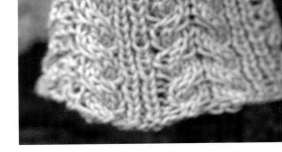

BACK

Using 2.75mm needles, cast on 119 [125, 132, 138] sts.
Row 1 (Wrong side) K2 [1, 2, 1], (p1, k1) 4 [6, 4, 6] times, *p8, k1 (p1, k1) twice; rep from * to last 5 [8, 5, 8] sts, (p1, k1) 2 [4, 2, 4] times, k1 [0, 1, 0].
Row 2 K0 [1, 0, 1], (k1, p1) 5 [6, 5, 6] times, *c4f, c4b, p1, (k1, p1) twice; rep from * to last 5 [8, 5, 8] sts, (k1, p1) 2 [3, 2, 3] times, k1 [2, 1, 2].
Row 3 As row 1.
Row 4 K0 [1, 0, 1], (k1, p1) 5 [6, 5, 6] times, *k8, p1, (k1, p1) twice; rep from * to last 5 [8, 5, 8] sts, (k1, p1) 2 [3, 2, 3] times, k1 [2, 1, 2].
Rep these 4 rows 7 times more, then work rows 1 to 3 once.
Next row K0 [1, 0, 1], (inc in next st, p1) 5 [6, 5, 6] times, *k8, inc in next st, (k1, inc in next st) twice; rep from * to last 18 [21, 18, 21] sts, k8, (p1, inc in next st) 5 [6, 5, 6] times, k0 [1, 0, 1]. *150 [158, 166, 174] sts.*
Change to 3.25mm needles. Commence patt.
Row 1 K15 [19, 15, 19], (p8, k8) to last 7 [11, 7, 11] sts, k7 [11, 7, 11].

Row 2 P15 [19, 15, 19], (c4f, c4b, p8) to last 7 [11, 7, 11] sts, p7 [11, 7, 11].
Row 3 As row 1.
Row 4 P15 [19, 15, 19], (k8, p8) to last 7 [11, 7, 11] sts, p7 [11, 7, 11].
Row 5–8 As rows 1–4.
Rows 9 and 10 As rows 1 and 2.
Row 11 K15 [19, 15, 19], *p2, ybk, sl4, yfwd, sl same 4 sts back on to left hand needle, ybk, sl4, yfwd – referred to as bind 4, p2, k8; rep from * to last 7 [11, 7, 11] sts, k7 [11, 7, 11].
Row 12 P14 [18, 14, 18], *cr3r, p4, cr3l, p6; rep from * to last 8 [12, 8, 12] sts, p8 [12, 8, 12].
Row 13 K14 [18, 14, 18], (p2, k6) to last 8 [12, 8, 12] sts, k8 [12, 8, 12].
Row 14 P13 [17, 13, 17], (cr3r, p6, cr3l, p4) to last 9 [13, 9, 13] sts, p9 [13, 9, 13].
Row 15 K13 [17, 13, 17], (p2, k8, p2, bind 4) to last 25 [29, 25, 29] sts, p2, k8, p2, k13 [17, 13, 17].
Row 16 P13 [17, 13, 17], k2, (p8, c4f, c4b) to last 23 [27, 23, 27] sts, p8, k2, p13 [17, 13, 17].
Row 17 K13 [17, 13, 17], p2, (k8, p8) to last 23 [27, 23, 27] sts, k8, p2, k13 [17, 13, 17].
Row 18 P13 [17, 13, 17], k2, (p8, k8) to last

23 [27, 23, 27] sts, p8, k2, p13 [17, 13, 17].
Row 19 As row 17.
Rows 20–23 As rows 16–19.
Row 24 As row 16.
Row 25 As row 15.
Row 26 P13 [17, 13, 17], (cr3l, p6, cr3r, p4) to last 9 [13, 9, 13] sts, p9 [13, 9, 13].
Row 27 As row 13.
Row 28 P14 [18, 14, 18], (cr3l, p4, cr3r, p6) to last 8 [12, 8, 12] sts, p8 [12, 8, 12].
Row 29 As row 11.
Rows 2–29 form bodice patt.
Cont in bodice patt until 4 patt reps in all have been worked, ending with row 29.
Rows 2–5 of bodice form yoke patt**.
Cont in yoke patt, work 4 rows.

Shape armholes
Cast off 6 sts at beg of next 2 rows. Dec 1 st at each end of next row and every foll alt row until 124 [124, 132, 140] sts rem. Cont straight until armholes measure 20 [20, 21, 21]cm, ending with a wrong-side row.

Shape shoulders
Cast off 9 [9, 9, 10] sts at beg of next 6 rows

and 8 [8, 10, 11] sts at beg of foll 2 rows. Cast off rem 54 [54, 58, 58] sts.

POCKET LINING

Using 3.25mm needles, cast on 20 sts. Beg k row, work 5cm in st st, ending with a p row.
Next row (K2, inc in next st, k2) to end. *24 sts.* Leave these sts on a spare needle.

FRONT

Work as given for back to **. Cont in yoke patt.
Divide for neck opening
Next row Patt 72 [76, 79, 83], cast off next 6 [6, 8, 8] sts, patt to end. Complete right side of front first. Patt 4 rows.
Shape armhole
Cast off 6 sts at beg of next row. Dec 1 st at armhole edge on next row and every foll alt row until 59 [59, 62, 66] sts rem. Cont straight until armhole measures 14 [14, 15, 15]cm, ending at neck edge.
Shape neck
Cast off 12 sts at beg of next row. Dec 1 st at neck edge on every row until 35 [35, 37, 41] sts rem. Cont straight until front matches back to shoulder, ending at armhole edge.

Shape shoulder
Cast off 9 sts at beg of next row and 2 foll alt rows. Work 1 row. Cast off rem 8 [8, 10, 11] sts. With wrong side facing, rejoin yarn to rem sts and patt to end. Patt 3 rows.
Shape armhole
Cast off 6 sts at beg of next row. Dec 1 st at armhole edge on foll 4 alt rows. *62 [66, 69, 73] sts.*
Place pocket
Next row Patt 17 [17, 24, 24], sl next 24 sts on to a stitch holder and leave at back, patt across pocket lining, patt to end. Cont to dec at armhole edge on next row and every foll alt row until 59 [59, 62, 66] sts rem. Complete to match right side of front.

SLEEVES

Using 2.75mm needles, cast on 54 sts.
Row 1 (Wrong side) K1, *p4, k1, (p1, k1) twice, p4; rep from * 3 times more, k1.
Row 2 K1, *c4b, p1, (k1, p1) twice, c4f; rep from * 3 times more, k1.
Row 3 As row 1.
Row 4 K1, *k4, p1, (k1, p1) twice, k4; rep from * 3 times more, k1.
Rep these 4 rows 7 times more, then work rows 1–3 once.
Next row Inc in first st, *k4, inc in next st, (k1, inc in next st) twice, k4; rep from * 3 times more, inc in last st. 68 sts.
Change to 3.25mm needles. Commence patt.
Row 1 K1, p1, (p4, k8, p4) 4 times, p1, k1.
Row 2 K2 (c4b, p8, c4f) 4 times, k2.
Row 3 As row 1.
Row 4 K2, (k4, p8, k4) 4 times, k2.
These 4 rows form patt. Cont in patt, inc 1 st at each end of 2nd and every foll 4th row until there are 114 [122, 122, 130] sts, working extra sts into patt. Cont straight until sleeve measures 44 [45, 46, 47]cm from beg, ending with a wrong-side row.
Shape top
Cast off 6 sts at beg of next 2 rows. Dec 1 st at each end of next row and every foll alt row

until 86 [102, 94, 110] sts rem, then on every row to 40 sts. Cast off 4 sts at beg of next 6 rows. Cast off rem 16 sts.

NECKBAND

Join shoulder seams. With right side facing and using 2.75mm needles, pick up and k 30 sts up right side of neck, 44 [44, 48, 48] sts across back neck, 30 sts down left side of neck. *104 [104, 108, 108] sts.*
Row 1 (Wrong side) K1, p2, (k2, p2) to last st, k1.
Row 2 K3, (p2, k2) to last st, k1.
Rep these 2 rows 3 times more, then rep row 1 again. Cast off in rib.

BUTTON BANDS

Buttonhole band
With right side facing and using 2.75mm needles, pick up and k 40 sts evenly along right side of neck opening. Beg with a first row, work 3 rows in rib as given for neckband.
Buttonhole row Rib 6, (cast off 2, rib 8 including st used in casting off) 3 times, cast off 2, rib to end.
Next row Rib to end, casting on 2 sts over those cast off in previous row.
Rib 4 rows. Cast off in rib.
Button band
Work as given for buttonhole band but picking up sts along left side of neck opening and omitting buttonholes.

POCKET EDGINGS

With right side facing and using 2.75mm needles, rejoin yarn to the 24 sts left on holder. Beg with 2nd row, work 8 rows as given for neckband. Cast off in rib.

FINISHING

Block each piece as given on page 139. Catch down pocket lining and sides of pocket edging. Overlap buttonhole band over button band and catch down at base of opening. Join side and sleeve seams. Sew in sleeves. Sew on buttons.

Fountain Lace Short-Sleeve Sweater

❄ MATERIALS

Yarn

4 [4, 4, 4] x 100g balls Patons 100% mercerised cotton 4-ply (330m/361yds), shade 1692 Cream

Needles and Notions

1 pair size 2.75mm; 1 pair size 3.25mm; Crochet hook size 2.75mm

4 buttons, 1.5cm in diameter

Special abbreviations

c6f Sl next 3 sts on to cable needle and leave at front of work, k3 from left-hand needle, k3 from cable needle

c6b Sl next 3 sts on to cable needle and leave at back of work, k3 from left-hand needle, k3 from cable needle

ch Chain; **dc** Double crochet; **yrh** Yarn round hook

❄ MEASUREMENTS

To fit chest 81 [86, 91, 97]cm

32 [34, 36, 38]in

1 Actual chest size 88 [92, 97, 102]cm

34¾ [36¼, 38¼, 40¼]in

Length to back neck 51 [52, 52, 53]cm

20 [20½, 20½, 20¾]in

Sleeve seam 9cm, 3½in

Tension

28 sts and 36 rows measure 10cm over stocking stitch on 3.25mm needles (or size needed to obtain given tension)

BACK

Using 2.75mm needles, cast on 101 [105, 109, 115] sts.

Row 1 (Right side) K1 tbl, (p1, k1 tbl) to end.

Row 2 P1, (k1 tbl, p1) to end.

Rep these 2 rows until rib measures 6cm, ending with row 1.

Next row Rib 3 [2, 1, 1], (inc in next st, rib 2) to last 5 [4, 3, 3] sts, inc in next st, rib to end. *133 [139, 145, 153] sts.*

Change to 3.25mm needles. Commence patt.

Row 1 (P2, k2) 3 [3, 3, 4] times, p2, *k9, p2 [3, 4, 4], k1, k2 tog, yfwd, k2, k2 tog, yfwd, k1, yfwd, sl 1, k2 tog, psso, yfwd, k1, yfwd, k2 tog, k2, yfwd, k2 tog tbl, k1, p2 [3, 4, 4]; rep from * twice more, k9, p2, (k2, p2) 3 [3, 3, 4] times.

Row 2 (K2, p2) 3 [3, 3, 4] times, k2, *p9, k2 [3, 4, 4], p19, k2 [3, 4, 4] times; rep from * twice more, p9, k2, (p2, k2) 3 [3, 3, 4] times.

Row 3 (K2, p2) 3 [3, 3, 4] times, p2, *c6f, k3, p2 [3, 4, 4], k1, k2 tog, (k3, yfwd, k2 tog, yfwd) twice, k3, k2 tog tbl, k1, p2 [3, 4, 4]; rep from * twice more, c6f, k3, p2, (p2, k2) 3 [3, 3, 4] times.

Row 4 (P2, k2) 3 [3, 3, 4] times, k2, *p9, k2 [3, 4, 4], p19, k2 [3, 4, 4]; rep from * twice more, p9, k2, (k2, p2) 3 [3, 3, 4] times.

Row 5 (P2, k2) 3 [3, 3, 4] times, p2, *k9, p2 [3, 4, 4], k1, k2 tog, (k2, yfwd) twice, k2 tog, k1, k2 tog, (yfwd, k2) twice, k2 tog tbl, k1, p2 [3, 4, 4]; rep from * twice more, k9, p2, (k2, p2) 3 [3, 3, 4] times.

Row 6 (K2, p2) 3 [3, 3, 4] times, k2, *p9, k2 [3, 4, 4], p19, k2 [3, 4, 4]; rep from * twice more, p9, k2, (p2, k2) 3 [3, 3, 4] times.

Row 7 (K2, p2) 3 [3, 3, 4] times, p2, * k3, c6b, p2 [3, 4, 4], k1, k2 tog, k1, yfwd, k3, yfwd, k2 tog, k1, k2 tog, yfwd, k3, yfwd, k1, k2 tog tbl, k1, p2 [3, 4, 4]; rep from * twice more, k3, c6b, p2, (p2, k2) 3 [3, 3, 4] times.

Row 8 (P2, k2) 3 [3, 3, 4] times, k2, *p9, k2 [3, 4, 4], p19, k2 [3, 4, 4]; rep from * twice more, p9, k2, (k2, p2) 3 [3, 3, 4] times.

These 8 rows form patt. Cont in patt until work measures 32 [33, 33, 34]cm from beg, ending with a wrong-side row.

Shape armholes

Keeping continuity of patt, cast off 6 sts at beg of next 2 rows. Dec 1 st at each end of next row and every foll alt row until 109 [115, 121, 121] sts rem. **Cont straight until armholes measure 9cm, ending with a wrong-side row.

Divide for back neck opening

Next row Patt 55 [58, 61, 61] sts and turn; leave rem sts on a spare needle. Complete right side of neck first. Cont straight until armhole measures 19cm, ending at neck edge.

Shape neck and shoulder

Next row Cast off 12, patt to end.

Next row Cast off 7 [8, 8, 8], patt to last 2 sts, k2 tog.

Next row K2 tog, patt to end.

Rep last 2 rows 3 times more. Cast of rem 7 [6, 9, 9] sts. With right side facing, rejoin yarn to rem sts, cast on 1, patt to end. Complete as given for first side of neck.

FRONT

Work as given for back to **. Cont straight until armholes measure 15cm, ending with a wrong-side row.

Shape neck

Next row Patt 45 [48, 51, 51] sts, cast off 19,

patt to end.

Complete right side of neck first. Dec 1 st at neck edge on every row until 35 [38, 41, 41] sts rem. Cont straight until front matches back to shoulder, ending at armhole edge.

Shape shoulder

Cast off 7 [8, 8, 8] sts at beg of next row and 3 foll alt rows. Work 1 row. Cast off rem 7 [6, 9, 9] sts. With wrong side facing, rejoin yarn to rem sts and patt to end. Complete as given for first side of neck.

SLEEVES

Using 2.75mm needles, cast on 75 sts. Work 2cm in rib as given for back welt, ending with row 1.

Next row Rib 3, (inc in next st, rib 2) to end. *99 sts.* Change to 3.25mm needles. Commence patt.

Row 1 P1, *k1, k2 tog, yfwd, k2, k2 tog, yfwd, k1, yfwd, sl 1, k2 tog, psso, yfwd, k1, yfwd, k2 tog, k2, yfwd, k2 tog tbl, k1, p4, k9, p4; rep from * once more, k1, k2 tog, yfwd, k2, k2 tog, yfwd, k1, yfwd, sl 1, k2 tog, psso, yfwd, k1, yfwd, k2 tog, k2, yfwd, k2 tog tbl, k1, p4.

Row 2 K4, *p19, k4, p9, k4; rep from * once more, p19, k4.

Row 3 P4, *k1, k2 tog, (k3, yfwd, k2 tog, yfwd) twice, k3, k2 tog tbl, k1, p4, c6f, k3, p4; rep from * once more, k1, k2 tog, (k3, yfwd, k2 tog, yfwd) twice, k3, k2 tog tbl, k1, p4.

Row 4 As row 2.

Row 5 P4, *k1, k2 tog, (k2, yfwd) twice, k2 tog, k1, k2 tog, (yfwd, k2) twice, k2 tog tbl, k1, p4, k9, p4; rep from * once more, k1, k2 tog, (k2, yfwd) twice, k2 tog, k1, k2 tog, (yfwd, k2) twice, k2 tog tbl, k1, p4.

Row 6 As row 2.

Row 7 P4, *k1, k2 tog, k1, yfwd, k3, yfwd, k2 tog, k1, k2 tog, yfwd, k3, yfwd, k1, k2 tog tbl, k1, p4, k3, c6b, p4; rep from * once more, k1, k2 tog, k1, yfwd, k3, yfwd, k2 tog, k1, k2 tog, yfwd, k3, yfwd, k1, k2 tog tbl, k1, p4.

Row 8 As row 3. These 8 rows form patt. Cont in patt until sleeve measures 9cm from beg, ending with a wrong-side row.

Shape top

Keeping continuity of patt, cast off 6 sts at beg of next 2 rows. Dec 1 st at each end of next row and every foll alt row until 51 sts rem, ending with a wrong-side row. Cast off

3 sts at beg of next 8 rows. Cast off rem 27 sts.

COLLAR

With right side facing, using crochet hook and beg at right corner of neck opening, fasten yarn to edge, yrh and draw loop through (ch made); work 52 dc (hook into next st, yrh, draw loop through, yrh, draw through 2 loops) to left corner, turn. Ch 1, (1dc into next 2 dc, ch 4, skip next 4 dc), rep 3 times, 2 dc, fasten off. Join shoulder seams. With right side of back facing, using 2.75mm needles, pick up and k 20 sts up left back neck and 38 sts down left front neck to centre.

Row 1 (K1 tbl, p1) to end.

This row forms rib.

Row 2 Rib 34 and turn.

Row 3 Sl 1, rib 9 and turn.

Row 4 Sl 1, rib 15 and turn.

Row 5 Sl 1, rib 21 and turn.

Row 6 Sl 1, rib 27 and turn.

Row 7 Sl 1, rib 33 and turn.

Row 8 Sl 1, rib 39 and turn.

Row 9 Sl 1, rib 45 and turn.

Row 10 Sl 1, rib 51 and turn.

Row 11 Sl 1, rib to end.

Cont in rib across all sts for a further 3cm. Cast off in rib. With right side facing, using 2.75mm needles and beg at centre front, pick up and k 38 sts up right front neck and 20 sts down right back neck. Complete as given for first side.

FINISHING

Block as given on page 139. Join side and sleeve seams. Sew in sleeves. Sew on buttons.

Classic Cotton Crew Neck

❋ MATERIALS

Yarn
7 [8, 9] x 100g balls Patons 100% mercerised cotton Double Knitting (210m/230 yards), shade 2702 Sky

Needles
1 pair size 3.75mm
1 pair size 4.5mm
2 cable needles

Special abbreviations
c6 Sl next 2 sts on to first cable needle and leave at back, sl next 2 sts on to 2nd cable needle and leave at front, k2, p2 from cable needle at front, k2 from cable needle at back
c4f Sl next 2 sts on to cable needle and leave at front of work, k2 from left-hand needle, k2 from cable needle
c4b Sl next 2 sts on to cable needle and leave at back of work, k2 from left-hand needle, k2 from cable needle
cr3r Sl next st on to cable needle and leave at back of work, k2 from left-hand needle, p1 from cable needle

cr3l Sl next 2 sts on to cable needle and leave at front of work, p1 from left-hand needle, k2 from cable needle

❋ MEASUREMENTS
To fit chest 86 [91, 97]cm
34 [36, 38]in
1 Actual chest size 98 [104, 110]cm
38½ [41, 43¼]in
2 Length to back neck 60 [62, 64]cm
23¾ [24½, 25¼]in
3 Sleeve seam 44 [46, 48]cm
17¼ [18, 19]in

Tension
19 sts and 27 rows measure 10cm over basket pattern on 4.5mm needles (or size needed to obtain given tension)
30 sts measure 10cm over honeycomb pattern on 4.5mm needles (or size needed to obtain given tension)

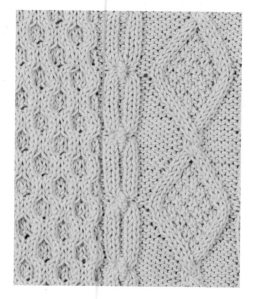

BACK

Using 3.75mm needles, cast on 88 [92, 96] sts. Work 7cm in k1 tbl, p1 rib.
Next row Rib 3 [2, 1], (inc in next st, rib 2) to last 4 [3, 2] sts, inc in next st, rib to end. *116 [122, 128] sts.*
Change to 4.5mm needles. Commence patt.
Row 1 (Wrong side) P0 [3, 3], (k3, p3) twice, k0 [0, 1], *(k2, p2) twice, k7 [7, 8], p4, k7 [7, 8], (p2, k2) twice*, p24; rep from * to * once, k0 [0, 1], (p3, k3) twice, p0 [3, 3].
Row 2 K0 [3, 3], (p3, k3) twice, p0 [0, 1], *p2, c6, p7 [7, 8], c4f, p7 [7, 8], c6, p2*, (c4b, c4f) 3 times; rep from * to * once, p0 [0, 1], (k3, p3) twice, k0 [3, 3].
Row 3 As row 1.
Row 4 P0 [3, 3], (k3, p3) twice, p0 [0, 1], *(p2,

k2) twice, p6 [6, 7], cr3r, cr3l, p6 [6, 7], (k2, p2) twice*, k24; rep from * to * once, p0 [0, 1], (p3, k3) twice, p0 [3, 3].
Row 5 K0 [3, 3], (p3, k3) twice, k0 [0, 1], *(k2, p2) twice, k6 [6, 7], p2, k1, p3, k6 [6, 7], (p2, k2) twice*, p24; rep from * to * once, k0 [0, 1], (k3, p3) twice, k0 [3, 3].
Row 6 P0 [3, 3], (k3, p3) twice, p0 [0, 1], *(p2, k2) twice, p5 [5, 6], cr3r, k1, p1, cr3l, p5 [5, 6], (k2, p2) twice*, (c4f, c4b) 3 times; rep from * to * once, p0 [0, 1], (p3, k3) twice, p0 [3, 3].
These 6 rows establish basket patt at each side.
Row 7 P0 [3, 3], (k3, p3) twice, k0 [0, 1], *(k2, p2) twice, k5 [5, 6], p2, (k1, p1) twice, p2, k5 [5, 6], (p2, k2) twice*, p24; rep from * to * once, k0 [0, 1], (p3, k3) twice, p0 [3, 3].
Row 8 K0 [3, 3], (p3, k3) twice, p0 [0, 1], *(p2, k2) twice, p4 [4, 5], cr3r, (k1, p1) twice, cr3l, p4 [4, 5], (k2, p2) twice*, k24; rep from * to * once, p0 [0, 1], (k3, p3) twice, k0 [3, 3].
These 8 rows establish honeycomb patt at centre.
Row 9 P0 [3, 3], (k3, p3) twice, k0 [0, 1], *(K2, p2) twice, k4 [4, 5], p2, (k1, p1) 3 times, p2, k4 [4, 5], (p2, k2) twice*, p24; rep from * to *

once, k0 [0, 1], (p3, k3) twice, p0 [3, 3].

Row 10 P0 [3, 3], (k3, p3) twice, p0 [0, 1], *(p2, k2) twice, p3 [3, 4], cr3r, (k1, p1) 3 times, cr3l, p3 [3, 4], (k2, p2) twice*, (c4b, c4f) 3 times; rep from * to * once, p0 [0, 1], (p3, k3) twice, p0 [3, 3].

Row 11 K0 [3, 3], (p3, k3) twice, k0 [0, 1], *(k2, p2) twice, k3 [3, 4], p2, (k1, p1) 4 times, p2, k3 [3, 4], (p2, k2) twice*, p24; rep from * to * once, k0 [0, 1], (k3, p3) twice, k0 [3, 3].

Row 12 P0 [3, 3], (k3, p3) twice, p0 [0, 1], *(p2, k2) twice, p2 [2, 3], cr3r, (k1, p1) 4 times, cr3l, p2 [2, 3], (k2, p2) twice*, k24; rep from * to * once, p0 [0, 1], (p3, k3) twice, p0 [3, 3].
These 12 rows establish cable patt at each side of diamond patt.

Row 13 P0 [3, 3], (k3, p3) twice, k0 [0, 1], *(k2, p2) twice, k2 [2, 3], p2, (k1, p1) 5 times, p2, k2 [2, 3], (p2, k2) twice*, p24; rep from * to * once, k0 [0, 1], (p3, k3) twice, p0 [3, 3].

Row 14 K0 [3, 3], (p3, k3) twice, p0 [0, 1], *p2, c6, p2 [2, 3], cr3l, (p1, k1) 4 times, cr3r, p2 [2, 3], c6, p2*, (c4f, c4b) 3 times; rep from * to * once, p0 [0, 1], (k3, p3) twice, k0 [3, 3].

Row 15 P0 [3, 3], (k3, p3) twice, k0 [0, 1], *(k2, p2) twice, k3 [3, 4], p2, (k1, p1) 4 times, p2, k3 [3, 4], (p2, k2) twice*, p24; rep from * to * once, k0 [0, 1], (p3, k3) twice, p0 [3, 3].

Row 16 P0 [3, 3], (k3, p3) twice, p0 [0, 1], *(p2, k2) twice, p3 [3, 4], cr3l, (p1, k1) 3 times, cr3r, p3 [3, 4], (k2, p2) twice*, k24; rep from * to * once, p0 [0, 1], (p3, k3) twice, p0 [3, 3].

Row 17 K0 [3, 3], (p3, k3) twice, k0 [0, 1], *(k2, p2) twice, k4 [4, 5], p2, (k1, p1) 3 times, p2, k4 [4, 5], (p2, k2) twice*, p 24; rep from * to * once, k0 [0, 1], (k3, p3) twice, k0 [3, 3].

Row 18 P0 [3, 3], (k3, p3) twice, p0 [0, 1], *(p2, k2) twice, p4 [4, 5], cr3l, (p1, k1) twice, cr3r, p4 [4, 5], (k2, p2) twice*, (c4b, c4f) 3 times; rep from * to * once, p0 [0, 1], (p3, k3) twice, p0 [3, 3].

Row 19 As row 7.

Row 20 K0 [3, 3], (p3, k3) twice, p0 [0, 1], *(p2, k2) twice, p5 [5, 6], cr3l, p1, k1, cr3r, p5 [5, 6], (k2, p2) twice*, k24; rep from * to * once, p0 [0, 1], (k3, p3) twice, k0 [3, 3].

Row 21 P0 [3, 3], (k3, p3) twice, k0 [0, 1], *(k2, p2) twice, k6 [6, 7], p2, k1, p3, k6 [6, 7], (p2, k2) twice*, p24; rep from * to * once, k0 [0, 1], (p3, k3) twice, p0 [3, 3].

Row 22 P0 [3, 3], (k3, p3) twice, p0 [0, 1], *(p2, k2) twice, p6 [6, 7], cr3l, cr3r, p6 [6, 7], (k2, p2) twice*, (c4f, c4b) 3 times; rep from * to * once, p0 [0, 1], (p3, k3) twice, p0 [3, 3].

Row 23 K0 [3, 3], (p3, k3) twice, k0 [0, 1], *(k2, p2) twice, k7 [7, 8], p4, k7 [7, 8], (p2, k2) twice*, p 24; rep from * to * once, k0 [0, 1], (k3, p3) twice, k0 [3, 3].

Row 24 P0 [3, 3], (k3, p3) twice, p0 [0, 1], *(p2, k2) twice, p7 [7, 8], c4f, p7 [7, 8], (k2, p2) twice*, k24; rep from * to * once, p0 [0, 1], (p3, k3) twice, p0 [3, 3].
These 24 rows form patt. Cont in patt until work measures 39 [40, 41]cm from beg, ending with a wrong-side row.

Shape armholes
Cast off 4 sts at beg of next 2 rows. Dec 1 st at each end of next row and every foll alt row until 92 [94, 98] sts rem. Cont straight until armholes measure 19 [20, 21]cm, ending with a wrong-side row.

Shape shoulders
Cast off 6 [7, 7] sts at beg of next 6 rows and 8 [6, 8] sts at beg of foll 2 rows. Cast off rem 40 sts.

FRONT

Work as given for back until armholes measure 11 [12, 13]cm, ending with a wrong-side row.

Shape neck
Next row Patt 34 [35, 37] sts and turn; leave rem sts on a spare needle. Complete left side of neck first. Dec 1 st at neck edge on next 8 rows. *26 [27, 29] sts.*
Cont straight until front matches back to shoulder, ending at armhole edge.

Shape shoulder
Cast off 6 [7, 7] sts at beg of next row and foll 2 alt rows. Patt 1 row. Cast off rem 8 [6, 8] sts. With right side facing, rejoin yarn to rem sts, cast off first 24 sts, patt to end. Complete as given for left side of neck.

SLEEVES

Using 3.75mm needles, cast on 42 [44, 46] sts. Work 7cm k1 tbl, p1 rib.
Next row Rib 1 [2, 3], (inc in next st, rib 2) to last 2 [3, 4] sts, inc in next st, rib to end.

56 [58, 60] sts.
Change to 4.5mm needles. Commence patt.
Row 1 (Wrong side) P0 [1, 2], (k2, p2) twice, k2, now rep row 1 as given for 3rd size on back from * to * once, k2, (p2, k2) twice, p0 [1, 2].
Row 2 K0 [1, 2], p2, c6, p2, now rep 2nd row as given for 3rd size on back from * to * once, p2, c6, p2, k0 [1, 2].
Row 3 P0 [1, 2], (k2, p2) twice, k2, now rep 3rd row as given for 3rd size on back from * to * once, k2, (p2, k2) twice, p0 [1, 2].
Row 4 P0 [1, 2], (p2, k2) twice, p2, now rep 4th row as given for 3rd size on back from * to * once, p2, (k2, p2) twice, p0 [1, 2].
Row 5 K0 [1, 2], (k2, p2) twice, k2, now rep 5th row as given for 3rd size on back from * to * once, k2, (p2, k2) twice, k0 [1, 2].
Row 6 P0 [1, 2], (p2, k2) twice, p2, now rep 6th row as given for 3rd size on back from * to * once, p2, (k2, p2) twice, p0 [1, 2].
These 6 rows establish patt for sleeve. Cont in patt as set, working appropriate rows of diamond and cable patt and working additional cable at each side of centre panel. Inc 1 st at each end of next row and every foll 5th row until there are 86 [90, 94] sts, working extra sts into basket patt. Cont straight until sleeve measures 44 [46, 48]cm from beg, ending with wrong-side row.

Shape top
Cast off 4 sts at beg of next 2 rows. Dec 1 st at each end of next row and every foll alt row until 58 [58, 62] sts rem, then on every row to 40 sts. Cast off.

NECKBAND

Join right shoulder seam. With right side facing and using 3.75mm needles, pick up and k 21 sts down left side of neck, 16 sts across centre front, 21 sts up right side of neck, 36 sts across back neck. *94 sts.*
Work 6cm in k1 tbl, p1 rib. Cast off in rib.

FINISHING

Block as given on page 139. Join left shoulder and neckband seam. Fold neckband in half to wrong side and slipstitch in place. Join side and sleeve seams. Sew in sleeves.

Shetland Lace

Along with the multicoloured knitting of Fair Isle, the Shetland Islands have produced world-famous lace knitting, which originated in the most northerly of the islands, Unst. The 'ring' shawls, knitted from 1-ply lace wool, were highly prized, and could take a whole winter to complete. So fine was the handspun wool that 57g of fleece could produce 5,500m of yarn, and the finished shawl was so delicate that, although perhaps measuring 2m square, it could be pulled through a wedding ring. The patterns were handed from mother to daughter, and combined traditional motifs such as Tree of Life, Spider's Web, Cat's Paw and Horseshoe. Lace shawls would be worn as a bridal veil and then used for christenings; black shawls would be worn for mourning. These are now museum pieces, and very few knitters remain who have the skill to knit them.

Commercial lace knitting in Shetland started around 1830 in order to provide employment when the first knitting machines, which could produce only a plain fabric, were introduced. The rise of this cottage industry was quite rapid, but it lasted only until the end of the nineteenth century. In order to popularize their lace, in 1837 the Shetland knitters presented Queen Victoria and the Duchess of Kent with fine lace stockings; shortly after this, a hosiery dealer introduced Shetland lace to the London market. Lace-knit underwear, stockings and children's dresses became much in demand, and every lady of fashion had Shetland lace in her wardrobe. A fine lace wedding veil was shown at London's Great Exhibition in the Crystal Palace in 1851, where the craftsmanship was greatly admired.

One of the reasons for the success of Shetland lace is the quality of the wool. The Shetland sheep is a small, hardy, and ancient breed; its wool has a long staple and is very fine and soft. In the summer, the fleece becomes loose naturally and can be plucked away or 'rooed' by hand. The handspun lace yarn used only the finest part of the fleece, from the animal's neck, making the lace light and delicate, but also warm.

The Shetland women themselves wore the plainer Shetland shawls, or 'haps', knitted with jumper wool, often in the undyed shades, with just a little openwork pattern in their striped borders. These were part of the crofting women's dress and would be worn with the corners crossed over the chest and tied at the back of the waist. This enabled the woman to walk around with her hands free to bring in the peat – or indeed to do her knitting.

The construction of the shawls is interesting. They are knitted from the edge inward, with as many edges as possible picked up from other edges, so that there are very few seams; those that do exist are made with a special technique in which the needle join imitates the join made with knitting. The finished shawl would be washed carefully and then 'dressed' by being strung onto a frame. In this technique, a thread is passed through the tip of each lace point and then round the numerous wooden pegs round the frame. After drying naturally, the shawl appears pressed to a perfect shape – and of course the same process can be repeated when the shawl next needs washing.

As the Victorian era came to an end, so did the demand for Shetland lace. There was a brief revival during the Second World War, when machine-made lace from Nottingham was not available because its factories were turned over to the production of munitions, and the Shetland knitters produced little lacy jumpers and cardigans to satisfy the demand. These garments – now so evocative of the 1940s – were often bought by servicemen stationed in the Shetlands, who sent them home to their wives and sweethearts.

All the patterns here are the traditional patterns knitted in Shetland for more than a hundred years; the one adaptation we have made is the New Shell sweater, which uses a traditional scarf stitch converted to a T-shaped garment in a jumper-weight yarn. Enjoy the warmth of Shetland wool and the soft colours of a very special area of Britain – these patterns capture a timeless style that is still totally wearable today. You will have created one of tomorrow's heirlooms.

New Shell Pattern Lace Sweater

This easy-to-knit pattern, with its pointed chevron effect, was traditionally used for fine lace scarves; here it has been adapted to the jumper-weight Shetland wool which corresponds to a 4-ply weight. The delicate pointed edging finishes off the sleeves and hem prettily.

Lace Cardigan in Eyelet Pattern

A traditional Shetland eyelet pattern is worked in 2-ply lace wool to make a gossamer-fine openwork cardigan, suitable for summer or evening wear. It is knitted in the round up to the armholes, making a virtually seam-free garment in this soft, light wool.

Old Shell Pattern Lace Sweater

This delicate openwork sweater is made from 2-ply Shetland lace wool. The shaded stripes of the natural colours of the famous Shetland sheep, combined with the lovely Old Shell pattern, make a timeless and classic sweater.

Fern Spencer

Traditionally a spencer would have been worn as an undergarment, but this one is much too pretty to be hidden away. Shown here in soft merino wool, it makes an easy-to-wear summer top. It is knitted in one piece up to the armholes, then the front edges are slipstitched neatly together.

Old Shell Shetland Shawl

The Shetland Islands have long been famous for their shawls, and the 'jumper wool' shawls often had borders using all the shades of the natural undyed wool. The border of this one features the Old Shell pattern and a pointed lace edging. Both light and warm, it makes a cosy wrap or pretty throw.

New Shell Pattern Lace Sweater

Yarn

Jamieson's Spindrift 2-ply jumper weight (100% Shetland wool, approx 105m/115 yards)

A 5 [5, 5] x 25g balls, shade 769 Willow
B 2 [2, 2] x 25g balls, shade 821 Rosemary
C 2 [2, 2] x 25g balls, shade 547 Orchid
D 1 [2, 2] x 25g balls, shade 562 Cyclamen
E 1 [1, 1] x 25g balls, shade 794 Eucalyptus
F 1 [1, 2] x 25g balls, shade 603 Pot-pourri

Needles

1 pair size 3.75mm
1 pair size 2.25mm

Notions

2 stitch holders

※ MEASUREMENTS

To fit chest 76 [81, 86]cm 30 [32, 34]in
Actual chest size 82 [90, 98]cm
32¼ [35½, 38½]in
Length to back neck 56 [58, 60]cm
22 [22¾, 23½]in
Sleeve seam 48cm, 19in

Tension

24 sts and 25 rows measure 10cm over pattern on 3.75mm needles (or size needed to obtain given tension)

BACK

Using 3.75mm needles and yarn B, cast on 101 [111, 121] sts. **Commence patt.
Row 1 (Right side) K1, (yfwd, k3, k3 tog, k3, yfwd, k1) to end.
Row 2 Knit.
These 2 rows form patt. Cont in patt and colour sequence as follows: 8 rows in B, 2 rows in F, 4 rows in E, 4 rows in C, (2 rows in A, 2 rows in D) 3 times, 2 rows in A, 8 rows in B, 4 rows in D, (2 rows in C, 2 rows in F) 3 times, 2 rows in C, 8 rows in E, 2 rows in D, 8 rows in C, 2 rows in B, 2 rows in C, 2 rows

in B, 2 rows in D, 8 rows in A, 2 rows in F, 2 rows in A, 2 rows in F**. Cont in A only until work measures 56 [58, 60]cm from beg, ending with a wrong-side row.
Shape neck
Next row Patt 37 [41, 45] and turn; leave rem sts on a spare needle. Complete right side of neck first.
Dec 1 st at neck edge on next 4 rows then on every foll alt row until 29 [33, 37] sts rem. Patt 1 row. Cast off.
With right side facing, sl centre 27 [29, 31] sts on to stitch holder, rejoin yarn to rem sts and patt to end. Complete as given for first side of neck.

FRONT

Work as given for back until work measures 52 [54, 56]cm from beg, ending with a wrong-side row.
Shape neck
Next row Patt 41 [45, 49] and turn; leave rem sts on a spare needle. Complete left side of neck first.
Dec 1 st at neck edge on next 6 rows then on every foll alt row until 29 [33, 37] sts rem. Cont straight until front matches back to shoulder, ending with a wrong-side row. Cast off.
With right side facing, sl centre 19 [21, 23] sts on to stitch holder, rejoin yarn to rem sts and patt to end. Complete as given for first side of neck.

SLEEVES

Using 3.75mm needles and yarn B, cast on 91 [101, 101] sts. Work as given for back from ** to **.
Work 8 rows in C, 2 rows in F, 2 rows in D, 8 rows in A. Cast off.

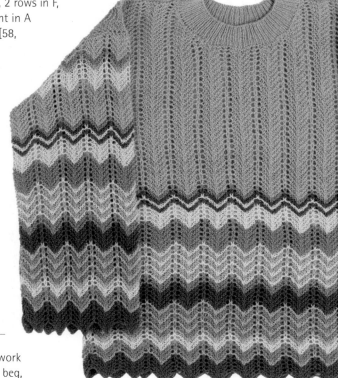

NECKBAND

Join right shoulder seam. With right side facing, using 2.25mm needles and yarn A, pick up and k 23 sts down left front neck, k across 19 [21, 23] centre front sts, pick up and k 23 sts up right front neck, 14 sts down right back neck, k across 27 [29, 31] centre back sts, pick up and k 14 sts up left back neck.
120 [124, 128] sts.
Work 13 Rows in k1, p1 rib. Cast off in rib.

FINISHING

Block each piece as given on page 139. Join left shoulder and neckband seam. Mark positions of armholes 19 [20, 20]cm down from shoulders on back and front. Sew in sleeves between markers. Join side and sleeve seams.

Lace Cardigan in Eyelet Pattern

POCKET LININGS

Using 3mm needles, cast on 21 sts. Beg k row, work 24 rows in st st. Leave these sts on a spare needle. Make another pocket lining to match.

BACK AND FRONTS

This cardigan is knitted in one piece to the armholes. Using 2.75mm needles, cast on 171 sts.
Row 1 K1, (p1, k1) to end.
Row 2 P1, (k1, p1) to end.
Rep last 2 rows 14 times then row 1 again.
Next row Rib 4, (inc in next st, rib 2) to last 2 sts, rib 2. *226 sts.*
Change to 3mm needles. Commence patt.
Row 1 (Right side) K2, (yfwd, k1, k3 tog, k1, yfwd, k2) to end.

Row 2 Purl.
Row 3 K3, (yfwd, k3 tog, yfwd, k4) to last 6 sts, yfwd, k3 tog, yfwd, k3.
Row 4 Purl.
These 4 rows form patt.
Cont in patt until work measures 15cm from beg, ending with a p row.
Place pockets
Next row Patt 8, sl next 21 sts on to a stitch holder, patt across sts of first pocket lining, patt to last 29 sts, sl next 21 st on to a stitch holder, patt to end. Cont in patt until work measures 38cm from beg, ending with a row 4.
Divide for armholes
Next row K2 tog, patt 47, k2 tog and turn; leave rem sts on a spare needle.
Complete right front first. Patt 1 row. Dec 1 st at beg of next row and every foll alt row until 22 sts rem. Patt 1 row. Cast off.
With right side facing, sl next 19 sts on to a safety pin, rejoin yarn to rem sts, k2 tog, patt 82, k2 tog and turn, leave rem sts on a spare needle. Complete back first. Cont straight until back matches front to shoulder, ending with a wrong-side row. Cast off.
With right side facing, sl next 19 sts on to a safety pin, rejoin yarn to rem sts, k2 tog, patt to last 2 sts, k2 tog. Patt 1 row. Dec 1 st at end of next row and every foll alt row until 22 sts rem. Patt 1 row. Cast off.

SLEEVES

Join shoulder seams. With right side facing and using set of double-pointed needles size 3mm, pick up and k 79 sts evenly around armhole edge, then patt across 19 sts on safety pin. Work in rounds as follows:
Round 1 Knit.

Round 2 (K3, yfwd, k3 tog, yfwd, k1) to end.
Round 3 Knit.
Round 4 (K2, yfwd, k1, k3 tog, k1, yfwd) to end.
Next round Patt 86, k2 tog, k1, k2 tog, patt to end.
Keeping continuity of patt, work 7 rounds.
Next round Patt 85, k2 tog, k1, k2 tog, patt to end.
Keeping continuity of patt, work 7 rounds.
Cont dec in this way on next round and 4 foll 8th rounds.
Next round Patt 80, (k2 tog, k1) twice. Sl last 2 sts of last round on to next needle.
Next round Sl 2, patt to end.
Work 6 rounds.
Next round K2 tog, patt to last 3 sts, k2 tog, k1.
Work 7 rounds.
Next round K2 tog, patt to last 3 sts, k2 tog, k1.
Rep last 8 rounds until 72 sts rem.
Work 7 rounds.
Next round (K2 tog, k1) to end. *48 sts.*

Change to double-pointed needles size 2.75mm. Work 32 rounds in k1, p1 rib. Cast off in rib.

FRONT BAND

Mark right front with pins to indicate buttonholes: first one to come 1cm up from lower edge and last one 7cm down from beg of front shaping, rem 4 evenly spaced between. Using 2.75mm needles, cast on 11 sts.
Row 1 K1, (p1, k1) to end.
This row forms moss st. Cont in moss st until band when slightly stretched fits along right front, across back neck and down left front, making buttonholes at pin positions as follows:
Next row (K1, p1) twice, yrn, p2 tog, k1, (p1, k1) twice. Cast off.

POCKET EDGINGS

With right side facing and using 2.75mm needles, rejoin yarn to the 21 sts left on stitch holder. Work 8 rows in moss st. Cast off.

FINISHING

Block as given on page 139. Sew on front band and buttons. Catch down pocket linings and sides of pocket edgings.

Old Shell Pattern Lace Sweater

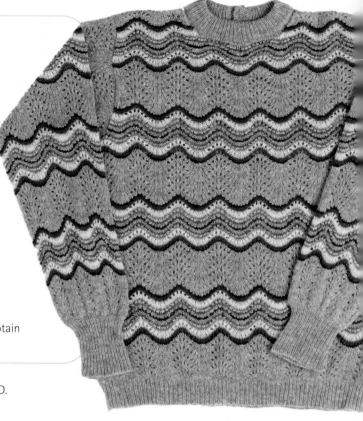

❉ MATERIALS

Yarn

Jamieson's Ultra 2-ply lace weight (50% lambswool/50% Shetland wool, approx 175m/160 yards)

A 5 [6, 7] x 25g balls, shade 103 Sholmit
B 2 [2, 2] x 25g balls, shade 101 Shetland Black
C 2 [2, 2] x 25g balls, shade 108 Moorit
D 2 [3, 3] x 25g balls, shade 105 Eesit
E 2 [2, 2] x 25g balls, shade 104 Natural White
F 2 [2, 2] x 25g balls, shade 107 Mogit
G 2 [2, 2] x 25g balls, shade 102 Shaela

Needles

1 circular needle size 2.25mm, 60cm long
1 circular needle size 3mm, 80cm long
1 set of double-pointed needles size 2.25mm
1 set of double-pointed needles size 3mm
1 pair size 2.25mm

Notions

4 buttons, 1cm in diameter
1 stitch holder

❉ MEASUREMENTS

To fit chest 76–81 [86–91, 97–102]cm
30–32 [34–36, 38–40]in
1 Actual chest size 90 [101, 112]cm
35½ [39¾, 44]in
2 Length to back neck 58 [61, 63]cm
22¾ [24, 24¾]in
3 Sleeve seam 53cm, 20¾in

Tension

32 sts and 38 rows measure 10cm over pattern on 3mm needles (or size needed to obtain given tension)

BACK AND FRONT

This sweater is knitted in one piece to the armholes.

Using circular needle size 2.25mm and yarn A, cast on 264 [288, 324] sts. Work in rounds of k1, p1 rib for 5cm.

Next round *Rib 11 [8, 9], pick up loop lying between sts and work tbl; rep from * to end. *288 [324, 360] sts.*

Change to circular needle size 3mm. Commence patt.

Rounds 1 and 2 Knit.
Round 3 *(K2 tog) 3 times, (yfwd, k1) 6 times, (k2 tog) 3 times; rep from * to end.
Round 4 Knit.

These 4 rounds form shell patt. Cont in shell patt and colour sequence as follows:

Rounds 5–18 In yarn A.
Round 19 In yarn B.
Rounds 20 and 21 In yarn C.
Rounds 22 and 23 In yarn D.
Round 24 In yarn E.
Round 25 In yarn D.
Round 26 In yarn F.
Round 27 In yarn D.
Round 28 In yarn G.
Rounds 29 and 30 In yarn A.
Round 31 In yarn B.
Rounds 32 and 33 In yarn A.
Round 34 In yarn G.
Round 35 In yarn D.
Round 36 In yarn F.
Round 37 In yarn D.
Round 38 In yarn E.
Rounds 39 and 40 In yarn D.
Rounds 41 and 42 In yarn C.
Round 43 In yarn B.
Round 44 In yarn A.

These 44 rounds form colour sequence.

Cont in shell patt and colour sequence until work measures 38cm from beg, ending with round 36.

Divide for back and front

Next round *Patt 9 and sl these sts on to a safety pin, patt 126 [144, 162], patt 9 and sl these sts on to a safety pin; rep from * once more.

Complete back first. Keeping continuity of colour sequence work backwards and forwards as follows:

Next row Purl.
**Row 1 Cast off 2, k7, including st used in casting off, *(k2 tog) 3 times, (yfwd, k1) 6 times, (k2 tog) 3 times; rep from * to last 9 sts, k9.
Row 2 Cast off 2, p to end.
Row 3 Cast off 2, k to end.
Row 4 As row 2.

These 4 rows establish continuity of shell patt. Keeping continuity of shell patt and colour

sequence, cast off 2 sts at beg of next 10 rows. Dec 1 st at each end of next row and 2 foll alt rows. 92 [110, 128] sts**.
Cont straight until armholes measure 15 [16, 18]cm, ending with a wrong-side row.

Divide for back neck opening

Next row Patt 42 [51, 60] sts and turn; leave rem sts on a spare needle. Complete right side of back neck first.

Cont straight until armhole measures 20 [23, 25]cm, ending at armhole edge. Leave these sts on a spare needle.

With right side of back facing, sl centre 8 sts on to a safety pin, rejoin appropriate yarn to rem sts and patt to end. Complete to match first side of neck.

With wrong side of front facing, rejoin appropriate yarn to rem sts, p to end. Work as given for back from ** to **. Cont straight until armholes measure 13 [15, 15]cm, ending with a wrong-side row.

Shape neck

Next row Patt 36 [45, 54] and turn; leave rem sts on a spare needle.

Complete left side of front neck first. Cast off 2 [2, 3] sts at beg of next row and 2 sts at beg of every foll alt row until 20 [29, 33] sts rem. Cont straight until front matches back to shoulder, ending at armhole edge.

Join left shoulder

With right sides of back and front facing, cast off 20 [29, 33] sts, taking 1 st from each needle and working them tog. Leave rem 22 [22, 27] sts on back neck on a spare needle.

With right side of front facing, sl centre 20 sts on to a stitch holder, rejoin appropriate yarn to rem sts and patt to end. Patt 1 row. Complete as given for first side of front neck.

NECKBAND

With right side facing, using circular needle size 2.25mm and yarn A, k 22 [22, 27] sts from left back neck, pick up and k 32 [34, 38] sts down left front neck, k 20 centre front sts, pick up and k 32 [34, 38] sts up right front neck and k 22 [22, 27] sts from right back neck. *128 [132, 150] sts.*
Work backwards and forwards in k1, p1 rib for 9 [11, 13] rows. Cast off in rib.

BUTTON BANDS

Button band

With right side facing, using 2.25mm needles and yarn A and beg at base of opening, pick up and k 26 [32, 32] sts along left edge to top of neckband.
Row 1 (Wrong side) (K1, p1) to end.
Row 2 (P1, k1) to end.
These 2 rows form moss st. Work a further 9 rows in moss st. Cast off.

Buttonhole band

With right side facing and using 2.25mm needles, rejoin yarn A to 8 sts on a safety pin at base of opening. Work 4 [6, 6] rows in moss st patt as given for button band.
Next row Moss st 3, cast off 2, moss st to end.
Next row Moss st to end, casting on 2 sts over those cast off in previous row.
Work 8 [10, 10] rows in moss st. Rep last 10 [12, 12] rows twice more then the buttonhole rows again. Work 4 [6, 6] rows in moss st. Cast off. Sew buttonhole band in position. Catch down button band on wrong side of base of opening. Sew on buttons.

SLEEVES

With right side facing, using double-pointed needles size 3mm and yarn A, k 9 sts from left-hand-side safety pin, pick up and k 108 [126, 144] sts evenly around armhole edge, k 9 from rem safety pin. *126 [144, 162] sts.*
Cont in rounds in shell patt and colour sequence as given for back and front. Work 44 rounds.
Next round K1, k2 tog, patt to last 3 sts, k2 tog, k1.
Patt 7 [4, 4] rounds straight. Rep last 8 [5, 5] rounds until 90 [90, 108] sts rem. Cont straight until sleeve measures 49cm. Change to double-pointed needles size 2.25mm.
Next round *K1, (k2 tog) 4 times; rep from * to end. *50 [50, 60] sts.*
Work in rounds of k1, p1 rib for 7cm. Cast off in rib.

FINISHING

Block as given on page 139.

Fern Spencer

❈ MATERIALS

Yarn

6 x 50g balls Rowan 4-ply Soft 100%
Merino wool (approx 175m/191 yards),
shade 387 Rain Cloud

Needles

1 pair size 3.25mm
1 circular needle size 3.25mm, 60cm long

❈ MEASUREMENTS

To fit chest 81–86cm, 32–34in
Actual chest size 92cm, 36¼in
Length to back neck 55cm, 21¾in
Sleeve seam 45cm, 17¾in

Tension

21 sts and 34 rows measure 10cm over
garter stitch on 3.25mm needles (or size
needed to obtain given tension)

PANEL PATTERN

Repeat of 25 sts
Row 1 Knit.
Row 2 and every foll alt row Knit.
Row 3 K10, k2 tog, yfwd, k1, yfwd, k2 tog, k10.
Row 5 K9, k2 tog, yfwd, k3, yfwd, k2 tog, k9.
Row 7 K8, (k2 tog, yfwd) twice, k1, (yfwd, k2 tog) twice, k8.
Row 9 K7, (k2 tog, yfwd) twice, k3, (yfwd, k2 tog) twice, k7.
Row 11 K6, (k2 tog, yfwd) 3 times, k1, (yfwd, k2 tog) 3 times, k6.
Row 13 K5, (k2 tog, yfwd) 3 times, k3, (yfwd, k2 tog) 3 times, k5.
Row 15 K4, (k2 tog, yfwd) 4 times, k1, (yfwd, k2 tog) 4 times, k4.
Row 17 K3, (k2 tog, yfwd) 4 times, k3, (yfwd, k2 tog) 4 times, k3.
Row 19 K2, (k2 tog, yfwd) 5 times, k1, (yfwd, k2 tog) 5 times, k2.
Row 21 As row 17.
Row 23 As row 15.
Row 25 As row 13.
Row 27 As row 11.
Row 29 As row 9.
Row 31 As row 7.
Row 33 As row 5.
Row 35 K11, yfwd, k3 tog, yfwd, k11.
Row 36 Knit.
These 36 rows form panel patt.

BACK AND FRONT

This sweater is worked in one piece to the armholes. Using 3.25mm needles, cast on 143 sts.
Knit 1 row.
Row 1 K2, (yfwd, k3, k3 tog, k3, yfwd, k1) to last st, k1.
Row 2 Knit.
These 2 rows form welt patt. Rep these 2 rows 9 times.
Next row K15, (k2 tog, k26) 4 times, k2 tog, k14. *138 sts.*
Knit 1 row.
Next row K1, (yfwd, k 2 tog) to last st, yfwd, k1. *139 sts.*
Knit 1 row. Cont in patt as follows:
Row 1 Knit.
Row 2 and every foll alt row Knit.
Row 3 Work row 3 of panel patt, k1, yfwd, k16, yfwd, k to last 42 sts, yfwd, k16, yfwd, k1, work row 3 of panel patt.
Row 5 Work row 5 of panel patt, k to last 25 sts, work row 5 of panel patt.
Row 7 Work row 7 of panel patt, k to last 25 sts, work row 7 of panel patt.
Row 9 Work row 9 of panel patt, k to last 25 sts, work row 9 of panel patt.
Row 11 Work row 11 of panel patt, k2, yfwd, k16, yfwd, k to last 43 sts, yfwd, k16, yfwd, k2, work row 11 of panel patt.
Cont in this way, working appropriate rows of panel patt and inc sts as set on every foll 8th row until there are 195 sts. Work 1 row.

Divide for armholes

Next row K2, k2 tog, yfwd, k1, k2 tog, k34 and turn; leave rem sts on a spare needle. Complete right side of neck first.
Row 1 K to last 4 sts, yfwd, k2 tog, k2.
Row 2 K2, k2 tog, yfwd, k to end.
Rows 3 and 4 As rows 1 and 2.
Row 5 As row 1.
Row 6 K2, k2 tog, yfwd, k1, k2 tog, k to end.
Rep these 6 rows 7 times then rows 1 and 2 again. Cast off rem 32 sts.
With right side facing, sl next 15 sts on to a safety pin, rejoin yarn to rem sts, k83 and turn; leave rem sts on a spare needle. Knit 49 rows.

Shape shoulders

Cast off 28 sts at beg of next 2 rows. *27 sts.*
Next row K1, (yfwd, k2 tog) to end.
Knit 3 rows. Cast off.
With right side facing, sl next 15 sts on to a safety pin, rejoin yarn to rem sts, k to last 7 sts, k2 tog, k1, yfwd, k2 tog, k2.
Row 1 K2, k2 tog, yfwd, k to end.
Row 2 K to last 4 sts, yfwd, k2 tog, k2.
Rows 3 and 4 As rows 1 and 2.

Row 5 As row 1.
Row 6 K to last 7 sts, k2 tog, k1, yfwd, k2 tog, k2.
Rep these 6 rows 7 times then row 1 again.
Cast off rem 32 sts.

SLEEVES

Join shoulder and neck edge border seams.

With right side facing and using circular needle size 3.25mm, k7 sts from safety pin, pick up and k 52 sts evenly around armhole edge, then k rem 8 sts on safety pin. *67 sts*. Work backwards and forwards. K 57 rows.
Next row K2 tog, k to last 3 sts, k2 tog, k1. K 7 rows straight. Rep last 8 rows 7 times.
Next row K2tog, k to last 3 sts, k2 tog. k1. K 3 rows straight. Rep last 4 rows 3 times. *43 sts*. Work 12 rows in welt patt as given for main part. Cast off.

FINISHING

Block as given on page 139. Join centre front and sleeve seams.

Old Shell Shetland Shawl

Special note

This shawl is knitted in sections as follows:
Part 1 The scalloped lace edging that goes
around two sides.
Part 2 The striped border for two sides with
Old Shell pattern and with an openwork stitch
at centre of rows (ie dividing the two sides)
and one end of the rows.
Parts 3 and 4 As parts 1 and 2, to make the
edging and border for the other two sides.
Part 5 The centre panel, which is worked from
the inside edge of half of one of the border
pieces (ie one side of the shawl), knitting in
the other half of the same border piece, and
half of the other border piece.

SCALLOPED LACE EDGING

This is part 1 on the diagram.
Using 5mm needles and yarn A cast on 6 sts.
Row 1 K4, yfwd, k2.
Row 2 K2, yfwd, k5.
Row 3 K6, yfwd, k2.
Row 4 K2, yfwd, k7.
Row 5 K8, yfwd, k2.
Row 6 K2, yfwd, k9. *12 sts.*
Row 7 K7, k2 tog, yfwd, k2 tog, k1.

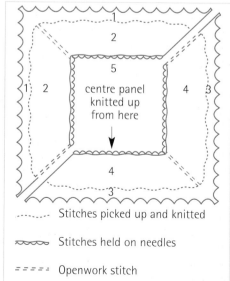

········· Stitches picked up and knitted

〜〜〜 Stitches held on needles

===== Openwork stitch

Row 8 K1, k2 tog, yfwd, k2 tog, k6.
Row 9 K5, k2 tog, yfwd, k2 tog, k1.
Row 10 K1, k2 tog, yfwd, k2 tog, k4.
Row 11 K3, k2 tog, yfwd, k2 tog, k1.
Row 12 K1, k2 tog, yfwd, k2 tog, k2. *6 sts.*
Rows 13 to 18 Knit.
Rep these 18 rows 28 times more, then work rows 1–17.
Next row Cast off these 6 sts, but do not turn and break off yarn.

STRIPED BORDER

This is part 2 on the diagram.
Change to yarn B. Pick up and k 270 sts along straight edge of work.
Next row (Wrong side) *K2, yfwd, k2 tog, k5, (k2 tog, k7) 14 times; rep from * once more. *242 sts.*
Commence patt. Change to yarn A.
Row 1 (K119, yfwd, k2 tog) twice.
Row 2 (K2, yfwd, k2 tog, k117) twice.
Row 3 **K6, *(k2 tog) 3 times, (yfwd, k1) 5 times, yfwd, (k2 tog) 3 times, k1, rep from * 5 times more, k5, yfwd, k2 tog**; rep from ** to ** once more.
Row 4 As row 2.
Change to yarn B.
Rows 5–8 Rep rows 1 and 2 twice.
These 8 rows form patt. Cont in patt and yarn sequence as follows:
2 rows in yarn B, 2 rows in yarn C, 4 rows in yarn B, 6 rows in yarn C, 2 rows in yarn D, 4 rows in yarn C, 6 rows in yarn D, 2 rows in yarn E, 4 rows in yarn D, 6 rows in yarn E, 2 rows in yarn B, 2 rows in yarn E, ending with a 2nd row of the patt.
Shape border
Cont with yarn E.
Row 1 **K5, (k2 tog) 3 times, (yfwd, k1) 4 times, yfwd, (k2 tog) 4 times, *k1, (k2 tog) 3 times, (yfwd, k1) 5 times, yfwd, (k 2 tog) 3 times; rep from * 3 times more, k1, (k2 tog) 4 times, (yfwd, k1) 4 times, yfwd, (k2 tog) 3 times, k5, yfwd, k2 tog**; rep from ** to ** once more. *234 sts.*
Row 2 (K2, yfwd, k2 tog, k113) twice.
Change to yarn B.
Row 3 (K115, yfwd, k2 tog) twice.
Row 4 As row 2.

Rows 5 to 8 Rep rows 3 and 4 twice.
Change to yarn C.
Row 9 **K4, (k2 tog) 3 times, (yfwd, k1) 3 times, yfwd, (k2 tog) 4 times, *k1, (k2 tog) 3 times, (yfwd, k1) 5 times, yfwd, (k2 tog) 3 times; rep from * 3 times more, k1, (k2 tog) 4 times, (yfwd, k1) 3 times, yfwd, (k2 tog) 3 times, k4, yfwd, k2 tog**; rep from ** to ** once more. *222 sts.*
Row 10 (K2, yfwd, k2 tog, k107) twice.
Change to yarn B.
Row 11 (K109, yfwd, k2 tog) twice.
Row 12 As row 10.
Rows 13 and 14 As rows 11 and 12.
Change to yarn C
Rows 15 and 16 Rep rows 11 and 12.
Row 17 **K3, (k2 tog) 3 times, (yfwd, k1) twice, yfwd, (k2 tog) twice, k3 tog, *k1, (k2 tog) 3 times, (yfwd, k1) 5 times, yfwd, (k2 tog) 3 times; rep from * 3 times more, k1, k3 tog, (k2 tog) twice, (yfwd, k1) twice, yfwd, (k2 tog) 3 times, k3, yfwd, k2 tog**; rep from ** to ** once more. *206 sts.*
Row 18 (K2, yfwd, k2 tog, k99) twice.
Change to yarn F.
Row 19 (K101, yfwd, k2 tog) twice.
Row 20 As row 18.
Change to yarn D.
Rows 21 and 22 Rep rows 19 and 20.
Change to yarn C.
Rows 23 and 24 Rep rows 19 and 20.
Row 25 **K3, (k2 tog) 3 times, yfwd, k1, yfwd, (k2 tog) twice, *k1, (k2 tog) 3 times, (yfwd, k1) 5 times, yfwd, (k2 tog) 3 times; rep from * 3 times more, k1 (k2 tog) twice, yfwd, k1, yfwd, (k2 tog) 3 times, k3, yfwd, k2 tog**; rep from ** to ** once more.
Row 26 (K2, yfwd, k2 tog, k93) twice. Change to yarn D.
Row 27 (K95, yfwd, k2 tog) twice.
Row 28 As row 26.
Rows 29–32 Rep rows 27 and 28 twice. Change to yarn E.
Row 33 **K3, (k2 tog) twice, yfwd, (k2 tog) twice, *k1, (k2 tog) 3 times, (yfwd, k1) 5 times, yfwd, (k2 tog) 3 times; rep from * 3 times more, k1, (k2 tog) twice, yfwd, (k2 tog) twice, k3, yfwd, k2 tog**; rep from ** to **

once more.
Row 34 (K2, yfwd, k2 tog, k87) twice.
Change to yarn D.
Row 35 (K89, yfwd, k2 tog) twice.
Row 36 (K2, yfwd, k2 tog, k42, k2 tog, k43) twice. *180 sts.*
Row 37 K2, (yfwd, k2 tog) to end.
Row 38 Knit. Break off yarn and leave sts on a spare needle.
To make parts 3 and 4 on the diagram, work another scalloped lace edging and striped border as given above. Do not break off yarn.

CENTRE PANEL

This is part 5 on the diagram. Use yarn E.
Next 2 rows Taking 1 st from sts on spare needle and next st on left-hand needle, k2 tog, k88, k2 tog and turn, k90 and turn.
Rep last 2 rows until 180 rows have been worked. With right side of centre panel and rem border together, cast off 90 sts taking 1 st from each needle and working them tog.

FINISHING

Join corner seams, matching stripes. Block as given on page 139, placing a pin in each of the points of the lace edging.

Techniques

Measuring your tension

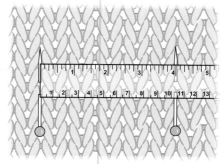

Measuring the number of stitches

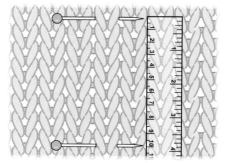

Measuring the number of rows

TENSION

At the beginning of every pattern is a
tension measurement, such as 22 sts and
30 rows measure 10cm over stocking stitch
on 4mm needles. This tells you how large
the stitches are on the garment so that,
by matching this tension, you can produce
a garment of the correct size. Four factors
affect the tension: needle size, stitch pattern,
the yarn, and the knitter.
Needle size Larger needles produce larger
stitches and smaller needles produce
smaller stitches.
Stitch pattern Different stitch patterns produce
different tensions; therefore you must check
your tension each time you embark on a new
pattern, using the stitch pattern specified.
Yarn Patterns worked in finer yarns have
more stitches and rows over 10cm than those
in thicker yarns. It is very important to che
ck your tension if you use a different yarn
from that specified in the pattern, as even
a standard weight of yarn can vary from one
manufacturer to another.
The knitter Even when using the same yarn,
needle size, and stitch pattern, two knitters
may not produce knitting at the same tension.

If your tension does not match that given
in the pattern, you should change to a larger
or smaller needle size.

Making a tension sample

Using the yarn, needles and stitch pattern
called for, knit a sample slightly larger than
10cm square. Block the sample as the finished
garment would be blocked.

Being careful not to stretch it, place the
sample right side up on a flat surface and
place a ruler along one row. Use pins to mark
the beginning and end of a 10cm measurement.

Count the number of stitches between the pins.
Then place the ruler vertically along one
side of a column of stitches, and mark your
10cm measurement as before. Count the
number of rows between the pins.

If you have fewer stitches and rows than
given in the pattern, you should use a smaller
needle; if more stitches and rows then you
should try a larger needle.

As a rough guide, changing the needle one
size makes a difference of about one stitch
in every 5cm.

If you cannot match both the stitch and row
tension, work to the correct stitch tension, as
the length can be adjusted by working more
or fewer rows.

SPECIAL TECHNIQUES

Some of the patterns in this book require
you to knit in the round, with circular or
double-pointed needles, to knit cables, to
follow colour charts, or to knit with two
colours of yarn in a row. Here is some helpful
information on these techniques.

Knitting in the round

Traditional Fair Isle garments, and fisher
ganseys are knitted in the round. This has

Knitting in the round

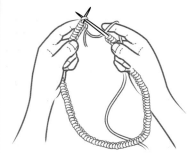

Using a circular needle

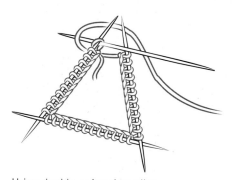

Using double-pointed needles

the advantage that there is much less sewing to do at the finishing stage. Also, the front of the work always faces you, so it is easier to follow the colour or stitch pattern charts.

Circular needles are used from the beginning when knitting these garments, but a set of double-pointed needles is more useful when picking up stitches, such as for necklines or sleeves.

To mark so-called 'seam' lines at every half round of a garment, use a small marker of contrasting thread. This will guide you when you have to divide for the front and back. Seam lines on ganseys are often indicated by a column of purl stitches in the pattern.

If you are using circular needles, you cast on in the usual way and knit into the first stitch to make a continuous round. You must make certain that your cast-on row is not twisted when beginning your first round. To knit stocking stitch, simply knit every row.

If you are using a set of four double-pointed needles, the stitches are divided among three of the needles, and the fourth is used to knit. To close the circle, knit into the first cast-on stitch, marking this stitch with contrasting thread, and making sure no gap forms in the knitting. If you find it difficult to avoid gaps when changing from one needle to another, you can rotate this point around the work by moving two or three stitches each time you change from one needle to another.

If you do this, it is important to mark your side stitches and centre back and front.

Stitch pattern charts

Simple patterns containing only knit and purl, such as those used on the fisher ganseys, can be shown on charts. In these, one symbol represents a knit stitch and one a purl stitch. When you are knitting in the round, the right side is facing, and the chart is read every row from right to left.

When the work divides at the armholes, and you are knitting backwards and forwards, you must read the first and all odd-numbered rows from right to left, and the second and all even-numbered rows from left to right.

Because the chart represents the right side of the work, all the wrong-side rows must be worked with the knit stitches being worked as purl, and purl stitches as knit.

Cables

A distinctive characteristic of Aran sweaters is the use of cables. These are created when stitches are moved out of position so that plaited, rope-like twists are formed. This is achieved by using a special, double-pointed cable needle.

A given number of stitches are slipped onto the cable needle and held at either the front or back of the work. A number of stitches are then worked from the main needle, then the stitches on the cable needle are worked.

Stitches held at the front twist a cable from right to left when knitted off; stitches held at the back twist the cable from left to right when knitted off.

Stitch pattern chart

knit ☐   purl ☒

Cables

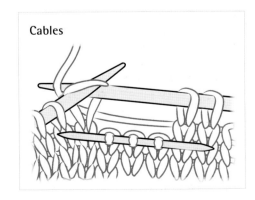

A typical colour pattern chart

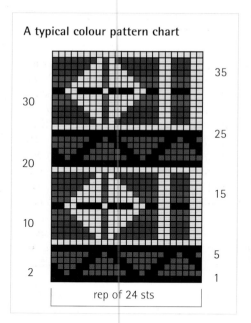

35
30
25
20
15
10
5
2
1

rep of 24 sts

Fair Isle knitting

In order to knit authentic Fair Isle, you need to knit in the round, follow a colour pattern chart, and use two colours of yarn in a row.

Colour pattern charts Colour patterns are often given in the form of a chart, where each square represents one stitch and each line of the chart, one row. In this book the colours are indicated by colours corresponding to those used for the garment, but sometimes they are indicated by symbols. The chart is worked from bottom to top, and the rows are numbered with odd numbers on the right-hand side of the chart, and even numbers on the left. The same chart is used for circular or flat knitting, although it must be read differently.

In circular knitting, every row on the chart represents a round of knitting. Since you have the right side of the work facing you, every stitch will be a knit stitch and you read every row from right to left. Mark the beginning of each round with a stitch marker.

For flat knitting, you will knit backwards and forwards in stocking stitch, so the first row (and odd-numbered rows) will be knit and the chart read from right to left. These are right-side rows. The second row (and every even-numbered row) is worked in purl and the chart read from left to right; these are wrong-side rows.

Using two colours of yarn in a row When knitting Fair Isle, the yarn that is not being used has to be carried across the back of the knitting. This is normally done by stranding; in Fair Isle there are not usually more than five stitches before a colour change, so there are no long loops at the back of the fabric. The advantage of stranding, as opposed to weaving yarns into the back of the work, is that the finished fabric is softer. However, it is very important that the strands at the back of the work are not pulled too tightly – both to achieve the correct tension (stranding too

tightly will pucker the fabric) and to produce natural give in the finished fabric. To ensure this, every time you change colour, gently but firmly pull back the last ten or so stitches on the right-hand needle so that your knitting is very slightly stretched.

Joining in new yarn Try to avoid joining a new ball of yarn in the middle of a round or row. To judge whether the remaining length of yarn is long enough to complete the round or row, use this rough guideline: in stocking stitch each round or row takes about three times the width of the knitting. In cable or texture knitting, the yarn needed is about five times the width of the knitting.

In Fair Isle, always join the new colour at the beginning of a round. Break off the old yarn, leaving a few centimetres of spare yarn; join the new colour and the finished colour with a single knot, making sure the knot is close to the last stitch on your right-hand needle. Begin the next round, and weave the spare yarn into the first ten stitches of the round, then carefully trim away the excess. This weaving can be done as you knit or at the finishing stage, using a darning needle.

If you have several colours joining in a short distance, it is easier to control exactly where they are worked in if you use a darning needle; run the end up or down the knitting for a row or two before darning it across the back of the work. This avoids too much bulk in any one row.

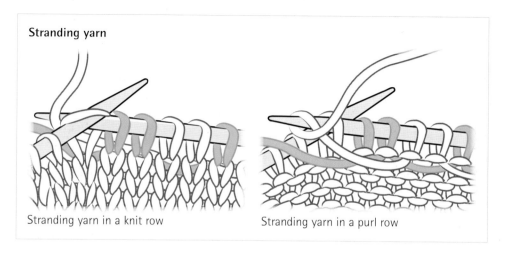

Stranding yarn

Stranding yarn in a knit row

Stranding yarn in a purl row

Sewing together – mattress stitch

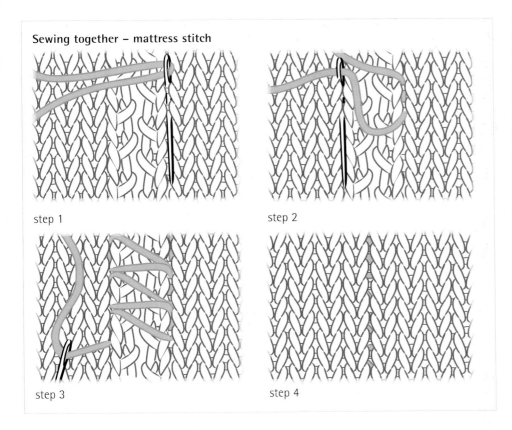

step 1

step 2

step 3

step 4

FINISHING

Blocking When you have finished knitting, the garment pieces have to be blocked and sewn together; if you have made the garment in one piece it can blocked in one piece. Pin the garment, or each garment piece, out on

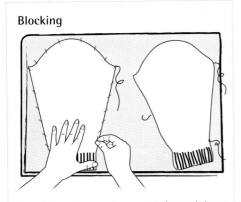

Blocking

Pin out the pieces to the correct size and shape

a flat surface to the correct measurements. The blocking surface can be a blanket or towel covered with a cotton sheet. Then spray the knitting with cold, clean water, using a plant spray, until it is just damp; leave it to dry naturally.

The fisher ganseys are not traditionally blocked, so whether you choose to do this is up to you.

For cotton garments, pin out each piece to size and then lightly press, using a damp cloth or steam iron. Do not move the iron across the fabric, but press gently with up and down movements.

Aran garments need only light blocking, because of their heavy texture. Pin the pieces out to size, spray lightly with water, and allow to dry.

The lace wool garments are delicate but do need careful blocking in order to obtain the openwork effect. In this case, dampen the knitting lightly, and on your blocking surface very gently ease it to the correct size so that

it is slightly stretched. Where there is a pointed edge, place a pin at the bottom of each point; allow to dry naturally.

Sewing together The ideal stitch for sewing up is mattress stitch, which provides a strong, invisible seam. Place the pieces right side up with the two seam edges side by side. Using a tapestry needle, stitch through two stitch bars, one stitch in from the edge on one side. Pick up the two stitch bars one stitch in on the other side. Without pulling the yarn taut, pick up the next two stitch bars on the first side. Then pick up the next two stitch bars on the other side, and so on.

When the yarn is looped from one edge to the other about five times, pull it taut to draw the seam together. Continue until the seam is complete.

For joining curved edges, as for a set-in sleeve, backstitch, as used in dressmaking, is most useful. Slipstitch is used for hemming neckbands in place and catching down pocket linings, for example.

Washing

After spending a lot of time and trouble hand-knitting a sweater, it pays to wash it with care. A lot of yarns now may be safely machine washed, so always check the ball band of the yarn for care instructions, and keep one band for reference.

Shetland yarns, however, must be washed by hand. Using a wool detergent, and hand-warm water, gently immerse the garment and squeeze it in the suds for a few minutes. Do not rub or soak it. Rinse in the same temperature several times to remove all the detergent and until the water is clear.

Place the garment in a thick towel and roll it up. Press the roll with your hands to remove as much water as possible. Alternatively, put the garment in a pillowcase and give it a very short, fast spin in a washing machine. Then spread it on a clean towel on a rack over the bathtub to dry naturally.

Guernsey-wool garments should be washed and dried in the same way.

Never hang knitted garments on a hanger, but always store them folded flat in a drawer or on a shelf.

Directory of Sweaters

Below is a directory of all the garments featured in this book, from chunky ganseys for cold days by the sea to delicate Shetland lace cover-ups. The soft, earthy palette used throughout has been inspired by the natural colours of the countryside.

Flamborough Fisherman's Gansey p30

Polperro Pattern Jacket p33

Newbiggin Pattern Sweater p36

Short-Sleeve Cotton Shirt p38

Jacob's Ladder Sweater p40

Fife Banded Gansey p42

Sanquhar Gansey p45

Eriskay Gansey p47

Caister Fisherman's Gansey p54

Cross and Flower Fair Isle Crew Neck p70

Cross and Square Fair Isle Slipover p72

Diamond Fair Isle Waistcoast p74

Katie's Fair Isle Slipover p76

OXO Fair Isle Crew Neck p78

Cable and Moss Aran Tunic p96

Chevron Aran Crew Neck p98

Tree of Life Aran Jacket p101

Wheat Cable Cotton Sweater p105

Fountain Lace Short-Sleeve Sweater p108

Classic Cotton Crew Neck p110

New Shell Pattern Lace Sweater p126

Lace Cardigan in Eyelet Pattern p128

Old Shell Pattern Lace Sweater p130

Fern Spencer p132

Old Shell Shetland Shawl p134

Directory of Sweaters   141

Stockists

CUCUMBERPATCH LTD

63 High Street
Wolstanton
Newcastle-under-Lyme
Staffs ST5 8BB
01782 862332
www.cucumberpatch.co.uk
For Rowan Yarns

FRANGIPANI

Caunce Head
Predannack
Mullion
Cornwall TR12 7HA
01326 240128
www.guernseywool.co.uk

IRISS OF PENZANCE

66 Chapel Street
Penzance
Cornwall TR18 4AD
01736 366568
www.iriss.co.uk/ganseys
sales@iriss.co.uk
for Wendy (Poppleton's) 5-ply Guernsey wool

JAMIESON & SMITH
(SHETLAND WOOL BROKERS) LTD

90 North Road
Lerwick
Shetland Isles ZE1 0PQ
01595 693579
www.shetland-wool-
brokers.zetnet.co.uk/index.htm
sales@shetlandwoolbrokers.co.uk

JAMIESON'S SPINNING (SHETLAND) LTD

Sandness
Shetland Isles ZE2 99PL
01595 693114
www.jamiesonsofshetland.co.uk
info@jamiesonsofshetland.co.uk

JOHN LEWIS

Oxford Street
London W1A 1EX
020 7629 7711
www.johnlewis.com
For Rowan Yarns

LOOP

41 Cross Street
Islington
London N1 2BB
020 7288 1160
www.loop.gb.com
For Rowan Yarns

ROWAN YARNS

Green Lane Mill
Holmfirth, HD9 2DX
01484 681881
www.knitrowan.com
For your nearest stockist

Acknowledgements

First of all, I would like to thank Jacqui Small, who chose this book to add to her craft list, and her team, who have brought this project to fruition.

Many thanks particularly to Margaret Stuart, in Shetland, who managed to find knitters still able and willing to knit up the Fair Isle and lace garments – they are now few and far between. Thanks to all the other knitters who undertook the projects against deadlines, who already have busy lives; and to Pauline Hornsby, who checked patterns when needed and helped to smooth out any little technical problems. It has been a pleasure working with everyone who has contributed to the finished book – it has rekindled many happy memories.

Madeline Weston

Knitters

Ganseys
Sarah Crowther
Abi Flynn-Jones
Jackie Hall
Pauline Hornsby
Helen Llamas
Margaret MacInnes
Lou Sugg

Fair Isle
Grace Anderson
Pearl Johnson
Barbara Reid
Katie Simpson
Julia Smith

Aran
Joyce Coombs
Sarah Crowther
Pauline Hornsby
Claire Hurley
Susan Smith

Shetland lace
Margaret Doull
Ina Irvine
Wilma Couper